CONTEMPORARY TEXAS

a photographic portrait

Bennie Peacock,
Foreman, Green
Ranch, Albany
Texas, June 1984

by Rick Williams

CONTEMPORARY TEXAS
a photographic portrait

MARTHA A. SANDWEISS, GENERAL EDITOR
ROY FLUKINGER, ASSOCIATE EDITOR
ANNE W. TUCKER, CONTRIBUTING EDITOR

ESSAY BY STEPHEN HARRIGAN

photography by

jim bones paul hester frederick c baldwin wendy v watriss mary peck michael allen murphy carol cohen burton rick williams

peter helms feresten stuart d klipper george krause ave bonar frank gohlke frank armstrong gay block skeet mcauley

TEXAS MONTHLY PRESS

Texas Monthly Press, Inc.
P. O. Box 1569
Austin, Texas 78767

A B C D E F G H

Library of Congress Cataloging-in-Publication Data

Main entry under title:

Contemporary Texas.

   Includes index.
   1. Texas—Description and travel—1981–   —Views.
2. Texas—Social life and customs—Pictorial works.
I. Harrigan, Stephen, 1948–   . II. Sandweiss,
Martha A. III. Armstrong, Frank, 1935–
IV. Texas Historical Foundation.
F387.C57   1986   976.4′06   85–12561
ISBN 0–87719–026–7

Printed in Japan by Dai Nippon through DNP (America), Inc.

Design by The Smitherman Corporation

This book is an outgrowth
of the
Texas Photography Project,
a program of the
Texas Historical Foundation
made possible by a generous grant
from the
Du Pont Company and Conoco,
its energy subsidiary.

contents

contemporary texas

In early 1984, the Texas Historical Foundation commissioned sixteen photographers to photograph the state on the eve of the Texas sesquicentennial. Normally, the foundation is concerned with the stuff of history, not with contemporary art. But historians traditionally take a long view of things and know that the modern soon becomes dated, the commonplace forgotten. Thus, as the foundation worked to compile a book of old photographs culled from collections around the state (now published as *Historic Texas: A Photographic Portrait*), it seemed appropriate that it should also work to insure that the Texas of today would be adequately documented. Ironically, though there are thousands or perhaps tens of thousands of snapshots made in Texas every day, there is no certainty that the Texas of 1985 will be as well documented as the Texas of fifty years before. Most color snapshots fade nearly as quickly

as the newsprint on which so much of our history is recorded.

Photographers were invited to participate in this project by an editorial committee of three: Roy Flukinger, Curator of the Photography Collection at the Harry Ransom Humanities Research Center, University of Texas at Austin; Anne W. Tucker, Gus and Lyndall Wortham Curator, Works on Paper, Museum of Fine Arts, Houston; and myself. There is no shortage of talented photographers working in Texas, and narrowing our choices to the photographers represented here was a difficult task.

We asked each of the sixteen photographers to submit a proposal for a photographic project that would document some aspect of Texas, hoping that the proposed projects would fairly reflect the diversity of life in the state. Happily, they did. The artists proposed to work in areas as different as the Rio

Grande valley and the Panhandle, the small towns of west Texas and the streets of downtown Houston. They proposed to photograph the petrochemical plants of the Gulf coast and the black churches of east Fort Worth, the state's business leaders and the ranchers of Albany. We accepted the photographers' proposals with only a few amendments and commissioned them to submit portfolios of ten exhibition prints each, along with contact prints and notes documenting all of the work they did for the project. Complete sets of the prints and notes compiled for the project are now on deposit at the Amon Carter Museum in Fort Worth and the Photography Collection of the Harry Ransom Humanities Research Center at the University of Texas at Austin; a partial set of exhibition prints is in the Museum of Fine Arts, Houston.

The 150 prints reproduced here represent sixteen (or perhaps fifteen, as two photographers worked as a team) discrete, personal impressions of Texas. As the photographers brought to their individual work a particular style and way of seeing, this book is less a systematic visual survey of Texas life than a series of vignettes or records of what was important to sixteen different people. The photographers all convey a powerful sense of place in their work, be it a place defined by land, work, culture, or imagination. And taken as a whole, the pictures suggest, even if they don't define, the patchwork of people and places and buildings that make up contemporary Texas. It is hard to imagine how one hundred and fifty pictures of a place as big and diverse as this could do any more.

Of all our advisors on this project, none has been as helpful as Russell Lee, a long-time teacher of photography at the University of Texas at Austin who surely knows more about photographic surveys of Texas than anyone else. He photographed in Texas as part of the great Farm Security Administration photographic project in the late 1930s, and ten years later traveled through the state taking pictures for the Standard Oil of New Jersey photographic project. Russell Lee generously shared his experiences with us and made valuable suggestions as to how to organize a photographic survey project.

Additional support for this project has come from Governor Mark White and his office and from Frank Calhoun, Brux Austin, Lynn Barnett, and John Ben Shepperd. At the Amon Carter Museum, Mary Kennedy McCabe helped prepare the photographers' resumes printed in this book, while Jessie Cartwright and Carol Roark also assisted with edi-

torial chores.

At the Texas Historical Foundation we've received help from Executive Director Leon Lurie and his predecessor Morrison Parrott, and from staff members Joanne Deaver, Tanya Fain, and Mark Trowbridge. Richard Pearce-Moses, the coordinator of the foundation's photography programs who expertly assembled and researched the pictures for the companion volume to this book, *Historic Texas: A Photographic Portrait*, also assisted with this project. And no editors could wish for a more supportive backer than the foundation's Vice-President, William P. Wright, Jr., who helped develop the idea for this project and imparted his enthusiasm to everyone who worked on it.

This project could never have come to fruition without the very generous support of the Du Pont Company and Conoco, its energy subsidiary. Their grant to the Texas Historical Foundation permitted the foundation to commission the work reproduced here and to deposit sets of the prints in the state's three major photography collections. In addition, the grant supported all of the research for the foundation's book on historic Texas photographs. At the Du Pont Company and Conoco, its energy subsidiary, our particular thanks go to Constantine

Nicandros, Gary Edwards, E. L. Lively, Ben Boldt, Perry McCahill, Eric Oshlo, Loretta Pittman, Sondra Fowler, and Tom DeCola. In every regard, the support of the Du Pont Company and Conoco, its energy subsidiary, has been a sterling example of enlightened cooperation between a corporation and a non-profit organization, and we are grateful to them for their support of the Texas Historical Foundation's photographic programs.

A traveling exhibition of the work commissioned for this project has also been made possible by a grant from the Texas Commission for the Arts, which awarded a grant to the Amon Carter Museum for the acquisition of a set of pictures that will travel around Texas during 1986, the state's sesquicentennial year.

Finally, thanks go to the sixteen photographers who participated in this project. All of them worked at less than their going rate in order to help get this project done. The other editors join me in thanking them for their hard work, their dedication, and their fine pictures.

Martha A. Sandweiss
Curator of Photographs, Amon Carter Museum
General Editor

measuring up to texas

Texas never quite disappears. It's like a distant star whose light keeps reaching us long after the source of that light has collapsed. Even so, there are many of us out there, born and bred, who cannot refer to ourselves as "Texans" without a beat of hesitation. Partly this is ironic distance, a sophisticate's acknowledgment of the various crude stereotypes the word calls to mind. But I think it is also a realization of the word's still powerful currency. When we call ourselves Texans, we had better mean it. And in contemporary Texas it is harder and harder to find the clear self-assurance that tells us we are worthy of the name.

Life in Texas was not always so ambivalent. Writing home to Connecticut in 1831, Mary Austin Holley reported that she had discovered a place where "artificial wants are entirely forgotten, in the view of real ones," where "delicate ladies find they can be useful, and need not be vain," where ordinary people "discover in themselves, powers, they did not suspect themselves of possessing."

If that is not the Texas we live in today, it is the one we believe in: a place that is not just a state of mind, not just the object of a droll and diluted allegiance, but actual earth and sky against which men and women test themselves and discover their "real" wants. It is a place that holds us to account.

Few of us anymore have that primal response to Texas. We do not understand the "land" as our ancestors did, it does not reside at the core of our self-awareness but simply serves as the ground upon which we conduct our lives. I know a woman whose three-year-old son asked one day to see where he had been born. She put him in the car and drove him to the hospital, only to discover that it had been demolished. Worried that her son would feel rootless without at least a building to claim as his point of origin, she drove past a shopping mall and told him that he had been born there.

Perhaps, when that boy grows up, his attachment to that mall will be as provocative and mysterious as, in generations past, it would have been to a plot of blackland soil or some hallowed rangeland his forebears had seized from the Comanches. The point is that Texas today is not necessarily diminished, it is just awesomely different.

My own experiences with Mother Texas have been spotty. I have a dilettante's love for the land but am at heart—like most Texans—an urban creature. A few days out of the year paddling down the lower canyons of the Rio Grande or wandering, parched with thirst, through the Guadalupe Mountains, are enough to sustain me in my illusion that I am somehow in contact with the silent directives of the haunted landscape.

But I did not rise from that landscape. I merely, from time to time, check in with it. I have no fealty to any piece of earth larger than a suburban backyard. I grew up in a boy's world of cowboy movies and cap guns, where bedspreads and lampshades were, as a matter of course, decorated with six-shooters and branding irons. Living in Texas, I felt uncomfortably remote from the image of Texas that kept pouring into my life. Where *was* this place?

The world I recognized and lived in day to day was ordinary. I found no wild fascination in it, but I was lulled by its petty comforts and the easy anonymity it seemed to offer. It was an urban world that did not challenge or provoke or demand payment. It was just a place, a place where I happened to live. There were horny toads in the backyard, dust devils and tumbleweeds in the vacant lots on the way to school, and sometimes arrowheads and bits of primitive implements in the creekbeds. I saw these things, looked for them, but by and large I lived in a Texas of the here and now, where the familiar crowded out the strange, where no one noticed the ghosts.

Like most Texans of my age, I have no faith in the endurance, the eternal vigilance of the land. I've seen too many roadcuts, too many cleared forests and strip-mined pastures, too many dried-up springs to believe it is possible anymore for the Texas landscape to leave its mark in the character of its inhabitants. Where that character still exists, the land is at its mercy. It seemed to me, when I was growing up, that the land changed every day without complaint. There was no scenery in that part of

Texas, no wilderness, just ragged wasteground waiting its turn to become part of the city. Nothing lasted; nothing was meant to. I remember how astonished a group of us were when, riding our bicycles on the outskirts of town, we came upon a cinderblock ruin, what remained of the concession stand of a drive-in movie theater. I crouched in the projectionist's booth, looking out its narrow slot onto a windblown field where a new subdivision was under construction. Nothing had ever felt so ancient to me as this empty building. I felt as if I had discovered the ruins of Troy.

No doubt, within miles of that place, there were things much older and more resonant waiting to be discovered: paleo rock shelters, untouched middens, bits and pieces of Spanish armor, hidden cliff faces decorated with Comanche pictographs. But I did not know of those things. I was a city-boy, the most casual sort of Texan (and now, I think, the most representative). It was not in me to understand something so primeval, to feel that blood-surge, that connectedness, with the past. I could only feel, hunched in that projectionist's booth, that something was missing.

Texas itself was missing from my awareness. It did not belong to me and I did not belong to it.

Texas was merely a fantasy zone of the public domain. When I was older I began to resent the distorted way in which my state was consistently presented to me. It seemed to be peopled only with back-slapping buffoons in Stetson hats, with mean sheriffs and spoiled women. There was the Big Land itself, eternally vigilant, eternally disappointed by the failure of these two-dimensional characters to measure up to its grandeur. The Big Land's hopes were pinned on just such a boy as I was not—the boy who sat solemnly at dusk on horseback, studying the distant buttes, who fought in the schoolyard to redeem the honor of his family name, and who snuck out of the house at night to keep company with his horse.

I resented those distortions but, like every Texan, I cultivated them too. Secretly I wanted the Big Land to watch over me, to judge my worth. An orderly urban existence in Texas seemed at times like an anomaly, even like a cruel joke, when measured against the tempestuous romance of the Texas myth. What kid, sitting in an orthodontist's office in the denatured heart of the Lone Star state, would not want to believe that some residual amount of that romance had found its way into his blood, and that it guided him like destiny?

"Contemporary" Texas is a place that is haunted by the past and by the excesses of its own self-regard. Sometimes it wants nothing more than to be perceived as an ordinary part of an ordinary world, and sometimes it demands to be Texas again, to be judged by a scale that is outsized and outrageous. The faint glimmer of that old image is important to us, and I suppose as much as anything it is the valence that holds us together, that lets us still think of ourselves as one particular kind of people in spite of a wealth of evidence to the contrary.

There are those of us who still trade somewhat on the myth in our everyday lives, and there are those of us who still live it, heart and soul. But for most of us it is an artifact, a beguiling little embellishment that never seriously distracts us from going about our business. We live in the big cities now, or in small towns filled with Walmarts and video arcades, where a restless young cowboy might rope a steer in the junior rodeo and finish out the evening by getting high and watching MTV.

Urban Texas is now official Texas, and one has only to watch *Dallas* to see with how much disfavor the world views that development. They see us as a throng of scheming oil men now. By moving to the city and turning our backs on the Big Land,

we have transformed our once-epic dreams into villainous bravado. We have rendered ourselves into spineless slugs who haunt Neiman-Marcus and sulk by the ranchhouse pool.

The real Dallas, of course, is much more intriguing. The specter of Texas may haunt its dreams, but the city does everything it can to obscure the fact. Driving through its streets, passing its art museums, its trade marts, its high-dollar punk clubs, you see a city with an almost desperate desire to be dynamic and worldly without the burden of being special. It's a city that in some complicated way is on the defensive. It wants you to know that it works on its merits, that it has nothing to prove. In its heart, perhaps, it wants to put the idea of Texas to rest, to become the greatest, most vigorous, most inspiring non-place in the world.

Dallas is a projection of every Texan's unsettled feelings about his state. We have to work harder at being cosmopolitan because our natural inclination is to be provincial; one of our bone-deep fears is that we will be perceived as a big state full of small-timers. In Dallas especially that fear is rampant: exorcising it is the first item on the city's psychic agenda.

Houston is famous for having no agenda, psychic

or otherwise. The city has no more motive force than a volcano. Unlike Dallas, whose poker face masks a hunger for acceptance, Houston is continually granting itself permission to be anything it likes. It is far from the most comfortable city in Texas and far from the most likable. There are some leafy glades around Memorial Park and Rice University, but otherwise there is little indication of natural works, no evidence to contradict one's initial impression that the city rests upon a native deposit of asphalt. In the summer that asphalt is as hot as magma, and the nearly liquid air droops and sags. And yet it is the most compelling city in Texas because its air of *not minding* is infectious.

I remember once being in the parking lot of a strip shopping center at the corner of Westheimer and Loop 610. I was about to get back into my car when I decided that I wanted to go across the street to the Galleria. This was a distance of about sixty yards, and it seemed absurd to take the car when I could just walk. But the street before me was invisible beneath an endless procession of automobiles, moving implacably forward in their legions. There was no pedestrian crosswalk on Westheimer, and as I tried fitfully to enter that solid chain of movement I could see the drivers staring at me with be-

wilderment, as if I were a moose who had wandered into the Houston traffic. Then it occurred to me: I was the first person ever to do this, the first pedestrian ever to be sighted attempting to cross Westheimer in front of the Galleria. I would have drawn less attention if I had been flywalking up the face of the Allied Bank Tower. In another city such a discovery would have filled me with remorse about the sorry state of civilization, but in Houston it made me feel like a pioneer, and when I reached the far shore I felt inexplicably warmer to this place. It is a city that is true to its own extremes.

Dallas and Houston stand at the poles of the Texas character. They represent the conflict between our genetic longing for an unruly wilderness and our dreams of a stable and accepted society. Houston, which never in its collective awareness gives the past a thought, is somehow a living museum of what Texans historically have been, just as Dallas is a preview of what Texans want to become.

Between those two extremes is the rest of Texas, the rest of us. Houston and Dallas are motivated by history, but it is a subliminal presence, a deep spring that seeps unnoticed onto the surface. In San Antonio, the spring flows. Driving along the loop, along the anywhere landscape of fast food estab-

17

lishments and motels, you can feel the gravity that the center of the city still exerts. San Antonio was there a hundred years before the anniversary we are observing in this sesquicentennial. In all that time it has been gathering the power of place until now it is as charged as a lodestone.

I could sense that power the first time I visited the city, an urban Texas boy with no sense of history, who had never seen a building older than the First National Bank. Standing in front of the Alamo, I was awed, as much by its appearance as by its bloody history. It looked so old to me I half-thought its origins were geological, as if it had long ago risen hissing and steaming out of the earth's crust.

San Antonio is like a Texas version of Jerusalem, a spiritual capitol that has been endlessly besieged and fought over but that in the end refuses to belong to anyone. It is the only city in Texas with that sort of self-possession, the only city with some grave and intoxicating secret at its heart.

That first sight of San Antonio convinced me, as much as anything has ever since, that Texas is not necessarily plain, that it is not just a drab flatland world endlessly compounding itself. It holds the potential for chaos, for unruly expression. Even in

today's Texas there is opportunity to find those "powers" in oneself that Mary Austin Holley spoke of to her friends back east.

Even when idly traveling through Texas, waiting in the loading lounge for a Southwest Airlines flight, or driving down 281 and listening to the middle-of-the-road country western stations flitting in and out of the car radio, I feel a charge to understand the place, because even if I do not unhesitatingly think of myself as a Texan I know that I am not really anything else.

Outside of the cities that charge is especially vivid. "Are we in the country yet?" my children ask whenever we leave our city en route for another. And every time they ask it seems like it is a little while longer before I can answer "yes." Cities no longer end in Texas, instead there is this vast intertidal zone between urban and rural, between past and present. As Texans, we are supposed to be citizens of both. But to us city-folk the "country" is an ideal: a silent, still, unpeopled place, dominated by lofty scenery, where we can count upon the hush of nature to quiet our souls. We have never worked the land; or, if we have, we have had enough of it. But it still taunts us. What good is a Texan without a ranch?

We make up our lapses where we can. We try to be complete. But even now when we are smugly urban and homogenized the variety of Texas life confounds us. What does a sawmill foreman in Diboll have in common with a Greenville Avenue boulevardier in Dallas? Does a black executive living in a mansion on Houston's McGregor Way think of himself as a Texan in the same way that a fruit picker in McAllen does, or a Vietnamese winner of a spelling bee in Port Arthur, or a bemused cowboy herding giraffes on the YO ranch?

All one can do, I suppose, is to try to bear accurate witness to the matrix from which all these contradictions spring. This book of photographs is about Texas today. There is no argument in them, no thesis. The project is just an attempt to do what has so rarely been done: to get the place right, to make it seem authentic and credible to those who know it best.

The sixteen photographers whose work is represented here went forth into the state with various creative fixations and ways of seeing, but they were under no instructions other than to take pictures of Texas. The images they have produced show a range of vision and expertise but also some consistency of attitude. There is a kind of wariness to these photographs, a cool and proper distance. You can sense the photographers' deep concern not to render Texas in the traditional yahoo fashion but to hold back somewhat, to study, to select.

It should be no surprise that the world they have recorded is largely an urban one, but what is unexpected to me is the cool regard in which the cities seem to be beheld. Paul Hester's photographs, for instance, show a world in which people are inert bystanders, no more substantive than the tiny human figures that are included for "scale" in architectural models. They are dominated by structures—arches and skylights and white vacant walls—that seem to have come into existence by their own accord. These buildings seem alive. They tolerate their human inhabitants but have no interest in them. One of the photographs shows a bare, high-ceilinged office, uninhabited. A pinstriped suitcoat is draped over a chair; a Coca-Cola can is on the cluttered desk along with a nameplate that says "James Randolf." The image is unsettling and creepy, because the room seems perfectly content without James Randolf in it.

It is an alien world that Hester describes. In one photograph a woman sits behind a desk in an office dominated by a model of the Transco Tower in a glass case, and you get the feeling that the thing seems to be living and breathing, and that when the woman turns off the lights and goes home the miniature tower will start growing like a beanstalk.

The same self-sustaining, inanimate objects exist in George Krause's work, although he seems to find them less threatening than Hester does. One of the most compelling of these images depicts a Houston skyline soaring above the tiny photographer. Elsewhere he studies the city at closer range, focusing on architectural details the way a nature photographer would focus on the bark of a tree or the striations in rock. The people in these pictures are impassive and unimpressed with this scenery, there seems to be a chasm between their own inner lives and their environment. The one notable exception is the smiling cowgirl opening the door to her white Cadillac, perfectly at home with any guise in which the state of Texas chooses to appear.

Skeet McAuley's people also exist in the shadow of an unnatural world, a world to which they have made a deadpan accommodation. Their work, glimpsed in disturbing fragments, seems to have something to do with maintaining and appeasing an invisible overseeing power. Workers in the Dallas Art Museum sweep up and punch a time clock in the intimidating presence of a giant stake driven through the floor. A man pours ink onto immense paper rollers that appear ready to ingest him. A woman with a fire extinguisher quenches a mysterious fire. Caught in these isolated stances, they appear trapped, in some sort of servitude that is far removed from the Texas ideal of self-reliance and freedom.

If people are insignificant in these photographs, in a number of others they are absent altogether. Stewart Klipper's panoramic studies of acid vaporizers and oil storage tanks are no surprise in this regard, since his painterly preoccupations with shape and form and color are so strong that living things would break the spell. Frank Armstrong keeps a formal distance too. He trains his camera naturally on lonely landscapes imperfectly redeemed by structures like gas stations and smelters and isolated churches.

Armstrong's structures, if you look at them long enough, manage to express something ill-defined but poignant, some wish in the landscape to lift itself up, to come to flower. Frank Gohlke's photographs share some of that poignancy. Everything here is vacant and expectant. A wading pool, filled to the brim, sits in the fading light of a Wichita Falls backyard. There is an empty playground, a peaceful stock tank, a bridge waiting to guide a traveler across the Red River. There is no starkness here, and you can sense an essential benevolence in the soft shapes made by willows and cedars, in the water that always seems close at hand and abundant.

Nobody is at home in Carol Cohen Burton's Texas either, but it's an utterly different place. Not morose, not haunted, it is filled with primary colors and quirky visions. It's a nothing place seen through a stylish eye. Mary Peck's eye is more severe. Black and white, made with a panoramic camera as if to emphasize how little there is to see, her Panhandle vistas have a hypnotic monotony. This is the land that nearly drove Coronado mad. In "Near Umbarger, Texas, 1984," Peck shows us a nightmarishly unmarked plain with a stand of trees far in the distance, a place of refuge that seems hopelessly out of reach.

Peck's powerful, relentless landscapes make one especially receptive to the work of a photographer like Jim Bones, who seems to glory in every detail of the natural world of Texas, the way every rock lies and every leaf floats on a pond. He has managed to impart an almost supernatural vividness and clarity to these photographs, to flush out every trace of color available in his subjects. Bones' vision of "contemporary" Texas is strikingly different from that of the other photographers in this volume, since it is the Texas that more or less always was. There is a completeness to it, and though we know better it looks as if it could not be disturbed. Bones' photograph of El Capitan and Guadalupe Peak, with its orderly field of boulders in the foreground, reminds me of the pictures of Mars sent back by the Viking lander—pictures that show a world so perfect in its stillness that it is immune to all depredations including time.

It is significant that, out of the one hundred and fifty photographs of Texas in this book, horses appear in only three. We see one horse from the rider's perspective, sighting down the animal's outspread ears at a pair of errant cattle. Rick Williams apparently took the photograph from the saddle—welcome evidence that at least one of our group knows how to ride.

Williams' pictures are ranch pictures. They chronicle a way of life that is both mythical and humdrum, that will continue to lodge at the root of the Texas identity however many light-years distant it may come to seem. His portrait of Bennie

21

Peacock is arresting not just for the way it evokes a particular individual but also for the way it confirms the existence of a legendary type. It could have been made a hundred years ago.

Another portrait of an enduring Texas individual is the one titled "A. V. Jones, Jones Oil Company, Albany, Texas." A. V. Jones may be a specific person, but anyone who has lived long in Texas knows the generic type he represents. This sort of Texan works in an office filled with manly trophies and knickknacks. He sits—when he sits—in a big leather chair, but he can't be still for long. In this photograph he has assumed a familiar posture: one fist resting on his hip, his other hand aggressively gripping the phone, his eyes peering over the rim of his half-glasses and studying something on the far wall—his daddy's shaving cup, say, or an original oil painting by D. B. Biddle called "Toughin' It Out." In this case—as evidenced by the livestock journals neatly spread on his desk by his secretary—he appears to be in the ranching business. He might just as easily be a maverick geologist, the owner of an oil field supply company, even a banker or lawyer. "Now dammit, Billy Don," he is saying into the phone, "Do we have a deal or not?"

Texas worships achievers. Michael Murphy has compiled a portfolio of them, the here and now of Texas iconography. They are the usual suspects— Ben Love, Michael DeBakey, Sally Ride, T. Boone Pickens with his monogrammed workshirt—but Murphy has managed to catch them in moments of unalloyed self-satisfaction, when they seem to be glowing with the knowledge that they have reaped the bounty of Texas largesse.

Success has been a more ambiguous phenomenon for the ten artists that Gay Block has photographed. A state that assigns automatic folk-hero status to its CEOs is not quite sure what to make of its artists, but the people in these photographs do not seem to mind. You can catch the outlaw glimmer in their eyes. Texas gives them something to play off against. My favorite among them is the portrait of Luis Jiménez, with his dragonfly t-shirt, sitting down to a plate of Mexican food and looking knowingly at the camera, perfectly content not to be president of Texas Commerce Bancshares.

It is sobering to turn from that photograph to Ave Bonar's portrait of two young Mexicans waiting to be deported. It is one thing to be cheerfully disenfranchised; it is another to be dispossessed. Bonar's work documents that strange region of Texas known as the Valley, where no valley exists, where denuded palms appear to have erupted out of the earth like spikes, and where the legend on a terrazzo walkway—"Paradise"—is sinisterly earnest. There is a gentle surreallism at work in her photographs—witness the "Woman at a Tea, McAllen, Texas, 1984," overwhelmed by her own elegance— and a social empathy that finds its strongest image in the deportation picture, with its hopeless bland room and circular mirror that hangs above the deportees like a bad moon. The two remaining groups of photographs are of black people, who have historically benefited so little from the Texas mythology that they have by and large paid it no heed. What is most remarkable about Peter Feresten's pictures from Fort Worth is their sense of community and ritual. There is a binding force here that might have something to do with Texas or might not, but it makes the "white" Texas we have observed seem fragmentized and uncertain. In the Ark of God, the Bright Glory Baptist Church, and the New Born Holiness Church, Feresten shows us people who make a point of keeping in touch with the ineffable. These Most Worshipful Grand Masters and Heroines of Jericho appear at times to be entranced by some over-arching and sure identity that other Texans can only envy.

The people in the photographs taken by Fred Baldwin and Wendy Watriss are more sullen and sophisticated. The tones are darker, and an air of purpose hangs over them. The people here are focused and ambitious. They want something more, and the photographers have caught them at moments of concentration and change. Unlike the blacks in Feresten's photographs, they look inward only to call upon their own solitary strengths. They are going out into the world. A boy says a prayer at a rodeo (another horse picture); a pool player, with fierce concentration, lines up a shot. And—in my favorite picture in the whole book—a bride leaves her parents' house, her eyes full of joy and foreboding. A true Texan, she leaves a safe and ordered world to confront her own frontier.

The photographers who made these images are no more certain of what contemporary Texas is, or what it means, than anyone else is. Most of them are Texans too, and just as bewildered and fascinated by our state as the rest of us. But all of them, I would guess, want that state to mean something. They want it to make them feel special.

The Texas the outside world imposes on us continues to be an annoyance, but we continue halfheartedly to accept it, because for now it is some-

23

thing to hold onto while we try to make sense of ourselves. My three-year old daughter, looking over my shoulder while I was reading a magazine, saw a tiny silhouette of the state and beamed with recognition. She had learned to identify it in nursery school. "Texas!" she shouted. "Look! It's Texas!"

And it was as if *that* were Texas, that little irregular shape. When her father hears the word "Texas," he thinks of a hundred things at once: a norther coming in over the Hueco Tanks, a long languid swim in the Shamrock Hotel pool, the sight of a wild orchid in the Big Thicket or a flock of sandhill cranes in Palo Duro, an astonishing snowfall on Corpus Christi Bay. But for her Texas is not a welter of experiences and images and contradictions, it is a little thing that floats across her mind and does not tax her understanding.

I hope it never does, but by the time she is old enough to ponder such matters Texas will be contemporary all over again, and that little shape may be all that is left of it.

When I think of the future of Texas I remember a Vietnamese housing facility I once visited in Missouri City, outside of Houston. It was a former summer camp that had been turned over to refugees as a place to help them effect a transition into a world most of them could not imagine.

A family had just arrived the day before. They were boat people. They had been captured by pirates in the South China Sea and escaped after a series of adventures that rivaled anything that LaSalle or Cabeza de Vaca had endured on the Texas coast. One of them, a little girl, was sitting on the stoop of a dormitory making a water buffalo out of Play-Doh. The rest of the family were inside, but they came out to be interviewed by a television news team. The family consisted of eight or ten members, and it was headed by an old matriarch who was carried piggyback by one of her grandsons. When he set her down in a chair near the swimming pool (which had been roped off for fear they would not comprehend its purpose and might accidentally drown) she looked at the TV crew with profound bewilderment and distaste. It was painful to see how strange this world was to her. She was like some burrowing animal that had lived its whole life underground and had been suddenly grabbed and hauled into the blinding light.

I think about her from time to time, wondering if she is still alive and wondering what became of her grandsons and the girl who was sitting on the stoop modeling a water buffalo. It is likely that they re-

mained in Houston, taking their place in the vast Vietnamese community there and slowly shaking off the shock of their new life. Perhaps no one has yet informed them that they are Texans, that their heirs can claim some strange and unfathomable alliance with the heirs of Charles Goodnight and Quanah Parker and Juan Seguin. If anybody tries to stop them, they have only to remind him that in contemporary Texas there is no such thing as a perfect Texan.

Stephen Harrigan

a
photographic
portrait

jim bones

For this project I proposed a view of the native lands of Texas, in a wild state, an image of old Texas as it might have appeared to the first settlers. As expected, with geological slowness, the waving grasses grow, clothing the rolling prairies. The caprock still crumbles, wasting the high plains. The Chihuahuan Desert advances up the mountainsides, replacing relic forests from the Pleistocene. Padre Island and its sandy associates shift with the longshore currents of the Gulf. Clear streams carve deeper into the fossil seabeds of the Hill Country, and the swampy woodlands go on building soil with their annual fall of leaves. However, as I crossed Texas on sprawling new highways, making these photographs, I encountered a difficulty I had not foreseen. Many of my favorite places have disappeared since I first looked closely, just ten or twenty years ago.

Change is natural, inevitable, desirable, but the rate of acceleration alarms me. For thousands of years before we came, Texas looked more or less unchanged, then in a little over a hundred years, it was largely cleared and domesticated. Each day whole communities of plants and animals, whose signatures are the very color of our lives, disappear, and hardly a year goes by that some creature does not become extinct. The individual deaths may seem imperceptible, but collectively they forever alter the face of Texas.

The remaking of this land in our own image strikes me, in a strange Orwellian way, like rewriting the history of life, while tearing out pages that led to this reality. How will our children know what made the cowboy's nomadic life so appealing without vast expanses to stand alone in, or what gave rise to the lumber baron's patronly wealth without primeval forests for shade, or what fostered the rich nautical traditions of the coast without clear bays or fish to catch?

Wilderness molded the lives of Texas' first inhabitants as it forged the myth that lives today. We are traditionally defined as a people by the way we make our bread and sew our clothes. But the earth first shaped our hands, even as we spun it into cities and industries and empires, and if concrete, glass, and steel supplant the wildland, our oldest heritage will survive only as heresay and pictures in books.

Texas has one of the smallest per capita systems of public lands in these United States, yet it would not take much to insure the perpetuation of its native places. A weed patch here, some vacant acres there, combined in a network of parks and preserves, primarily for the benefit of wild things, could provide a living gauge to measure the value of change itself. But that requires a change of heart that comes by understanding we are not separate from the plants and animals of the land that sustains us. We share the same helix of life, and when a piece dies, in a sense, so do we.

I hope the photographs from this project will stimulate a wider interest in the treasures we are daily losing, while casting new light on our origins, so the millenium just dawning will brighten on a land still loved and nourished by its people.

Jim Bones

Place of Birth: Monroe, Louisiana; November 1, 1943.

Residence: Santa Fe, New Mexico.

Education: Studied at the University of Texas, Austin, Texas, 1962–1967.

Professional Experience:

Teaching assistant to Russell W. Lee, Department of Art, University of Texas, Austin, Texas, 1965–1967; Production assistant to Ron Perryman, filmmaker, for H.E.W.-sponsored film, *Pandora's Box*, Austin, Texas, 1967; Research photographer and consultant, Programma de Education Inter-Americana, Texas A&M University, College Station, Texas, 1968; Career Fellowship, Environmental filmmaker-producer, Corporation for Public Broadcasting, KERA-TV, Dallas, Texas, 1970–1971; Photography teacher, Laguna Gloria Art Museum, Austin, Texas, 1972; Artist in Residence, Dobie-Paisano Fellowship, Texas Institute of Letters and University of Texas, Austin, Texas, 1972–1973; Printing assistant to Eliot F. Porter, Santa Fe, New Mexico, 1975–1978; Self-employed photographer-writer and wilderness guide, Santa Fe, New Mexico, 1975–present.

Selected Individual Exhibitions:

1965—Archer M. Huntington Art Gallery, University of Texas, Austin, Texas. 1968—*The New American Landscape*, Concordia College, Austin, Texas. 1976—Star of the Republic Museum, Washington-on-the-Brazos State Historical Park, Washington, Texas. 1978—Amarillo Art Center, Amarillo, Texas; Afterimage Gallery, Dallas, Texas; College of the Southwest, Hobbs, New Mexico. 1980—*Photographs from the Southwest*, Jerry Sullivan Gallery, Austin, Texas; *Western Rivers*, Nicolas Potter Gallery, Santa Fe, New Mexico. 1981—*Texas West of the Pecos*, Dallas Museum of Natural History, Dallas, Texas. 1982—*Mountains to the Sea*, Gallery 104, Austin, Texas; *The Rio Grande, Mountains to the Sea*, Nicolas Potter Gallery, Santa Fe, New Mexico. 1983—Museum of the Southwest, Midland, Texas.

Selected Group Exhibitions:

1976—f22 Gallery, Santa Fe, New Mexico. 1977—Santa Fe Gallery of Photography, Santa Fe, New Mexico; *Faces and Facades*, Polaroid Corporation, Cambridge, Massachusetts. 1978—*Southwest Fine Arts Biennial Exhibition*, Santa Fe, New Mexico. 1981—*Three Dye Transfer Printers* (with Eliot F. Porter and Peter Vogel), Graphics/Santa Fe Gallery, Santa Fe, New Mexico; *Two Views of Color* (with David Rathbun), Hill's Gallery, Denver, Colorado. 1982—*Santa Fe Festival of the Arts Photography Exhibition*, Santa Fe, New Mexico. 1984—*The Color Show*, Santa Fe Center of Photography, Santa Fe, New Mexico.

Books by Bones:

Texas Earth Surfaces. Austin, Texas: Encino Press, 1970.
Texas Heartland: A Hill Country Year. College Station, Texas: Texas A&M University Press, 1975.
Texas Wild. With Richard Phelan. New York: E. P. Dutton & Co., 1976.
Texas West of the Pecos. College Station, Texas: Texas A&M University Press, 1981.
Rio Grande: Mountains to the Sea. Austin, Texas: Texas Monthly Press, 1985.

Portfolios:

A Texas Portfolio. Eight handmade dye transfer prints. Austin, Texas: Encino Press, 1977.
A Wildflower Portfolio. Six handmade dye transfer prints. Austin, Texas: Encino Press, 1978.
Portfolio of the American West. For Southland Royalty Corporation, Fort Worth, Texas, 1979–1980.

Articles by Bones:

"Padre moods." *Audubon*, vol. 74, no. 5 (September 1972), pp. 64–71. (Portfolio)
"Riotous flora by a Texas wayside." *Audubon*, vol. 77, no. 4 (July 1975), cover, pp. 32–39. (Portfolio)
"El Despoblado." *Texas Highways*, vol. 29, no. 1 (January 1982), cover, pp. 18–23. (Portfolio)
"Running the Cañons of the Rio Grande." *Texas Highways*, vol. 30, no. 8 (August 1983), cover, pp. 20–31. (Portfolio)

"Out of the Old Rock." *Texas Highways*, vol. 31, no. 6 (June 1984), pp. 24–31. (Portfolio)

Articles and Reviews:

Asbury, Dana. "How They Work: 3 Master Printers and Their Assistants." *Popular Photography*, vol. 89, no. 12 (December 1982), pp. 79, 84–87, 172.

Pinkard, Tommie. "Dream of a White Christmas." *Texas Highways*, vol. 29, no. 12 (December 1982), cover, pp. 22–31. (Portfolio)

Photographs in Published Sources:

Fearing, Kelly. *The Creative Eye, Volume I*. Austin, Texas: W. S. Benson & Co., 1969, pp. 8, 11, 17, 19–20, 94. (Portfolio)

Fearing, Kelly. *The Creative Eye, Volume II*. Austin, Texas: W. S. Benson & Co., 1969, pp. 7, 13, 18. (Portfolio)

True West, vol. 17, no. 5 (June 1970), cover.

Old West, vol. 6, no. 4 (Summer 1970), cover.

Teale, Edwin Way. "Big Thicket: Crossroads of Nature." *Audubon*, vol. 73, no. 3 (May 1971), cover, pp. 12–32. (Portfolio)

Rugoff, Milton, Ann Guilfoyle, Ann Sutton, and Myron Sutton. *The Wild Places*. New York: Chanticleer Press, 1973, plates 85–90. ("Texas" Portfolio)

Frontier Times, vol. 47, no. 3 (May 1973), cover.

Hope, Jack. "Big Bend: A nice place to visit." *Audubon*, vol. 75, no. 4 (July 1973), pp. 36–49. (Portfolio)

Frontier Times, vol. 47, no. 6 (November 1973), cover.

Oberholser, Harry C. *The Bird Life of Texas*. Austin, Texas: University of Texas Press, 1974, pp. 20–21, 30–34, 36–37, 39–40, 43–46, 51.

Twelve photographic murals, permanent installation for *Lyndon B. Johnson National Historic Site*, National Park Service, Johnson City, Texas, 1975.

Reiger, George. "$25 will save a rhododendron." *Audubon*, vol. 78, no. 3 (May 1976), cover, pp. 46–55. (Portfolio)

Gruber, L. Fritz, Peter C. Bunnell, and Eelco Wolf. *Faces and Facades*. Cambridge, Massachusetts: Polaroid Corporation, 1977, pp. 51–54. (Portfolio of 8×10 Polaroid color prints)

Camera, vol. 56, no. 8 (August 1977), pp. 18–19.

Wolf, Reinhart. "Faces of Buildings." *International Photo Technik*, no. 1 (January 1978), pp. 40–41.

Harrigan, Stephen. "On the Edge of Texas." *Texas Monthly*, vol. 8, no. 4 (April 1980), cover, pp. 117, 120–121.

"The American Edge." *Audubon*, vol. 82, no. 4 (July 1980), pp. 57, 60, 75.

Deckert, Frank. *Three Steps to the Sky*. Big Bend National Park, Texas: Big Bend Historical Association, 1981, cover, pp. 6, 19–21.

Graves, John. "Big River." *Texas Monthly*, vol. 10, no. 6 (June 1982), cover, pp. 117–127. (Portfolio)

Evans, Karen. "Focus New Mexico." *New Mexico*, vol. 61, no. 5 (May 1983), cover, pp. 52–56.

King, Scottie. "Winter." *New Mexico*, vol. 62, no. 1 (January 1984), cover, pp. 14–15, 18–19.

Richie, Michael. "Farmington." *New Mexico*, vol. 62, no. 1 (January 1984), pp. 64–65.

Frantz, Joe. "On Boomtowns, Droughts and Water Pumps." *Texas Humanist*, vol. 6, no. 6 (July-August 1984), cover, p. 22.

Television:

North Padre Island, KTBC-TV, Austin, Texas, 1970.
Images and Memories, KERA-TV, Dallas, Texas, 1970–1971.
The Seasons, KERA-TV, Dallas, Texas, 1970–1971.
My Greatest Friend, KERA-TV, Dallas, Texas, 1970–1971.
A Song of Frogs, KERA-TV, Dallas, Texas, 1970–1971.
I Threw It All Away, KERA-TV, Dallas, Texas, 1970–1971.

Collections:

Alexander and Alexander of Texas, Inc., Fort Worth, Texas; Allen State Bank Collection, Dallas, Texas; Amon Carter Museum, Fort Worth, Texas; Greg Copeland Collection, Fairfield, New Jersey; Museum of Fine Arts, Houston, Texas; Photography Collection, Harry Ransom Humanities Research Center, University of Texas, Austin, Texas; Southland Royalty Company, Fort Worth, Texas.

bones

Sundown by the Rio
Grande, Sierra Vieja,
Presidio County,
1984.

All photographs are dye-transfer color prints.

bones

El Capitan and
Guadalupe
Mountains,
Culberson County,
1983.

35

bones

Eroded caprock and
brush, Palo Duro
Canyon, Randall
County, 1983.

36

Barton Creek, near
Bee Caves, Travis
County, 1983.

bones

Palmetto leaf,
Ottine, Gonzales
County, 1984.

Cypress Swamp,
Neches River,
Tyler County, 1984.

39

bones

Marshgrass and
cattails, High Island,
Galveston County,
1984.

40

Sunrise over the
Gulf of Mexico,
Padre Island, Kleberg
County, 1984.

bones

bones

Sand dunes and
shinoak, Monahans,
Ward County, 1983.

Autumn bluestem
grass, Decatur, Wise
County, 1983.

bones

paul hester

I intend these photographs to encourage thinking about the position of individuals within increasingly large concentrations of power. It is necessary to analyze the symbolic significance of the structures in order to understand the value system underlying their erection. The mass media contribute to our worship of these overwhelming totems but conceal the manner in which we are simultaneously tempted with the illusion of power and left powerless. It is my conviction that these photographs, while suggestive of the possibility of being seduced by the awesome, are more important as evidence of the need for social change.

Paul Hester

Place of Birth: Nashville, Tennessee; May 30, 1948.

Residence: Houston, Texas.

Education: B.A., Rice University, Houston, Texas, 1971; M.F.A., Rhode Island School of Design, Providence, Rhode Island, 1976.

Professional Experience:

Instructor, High School for Performing and Visual Arts, Houston, Texas, 1972–1973; Instructor, Dana Hall School, Wellesley, Massachusetts, 1976–1977; Photography coordinator, Media Center, Rice University, Houston, Texas, 1977–1979; Visiting critic, Department of Art, University of Houston, Houston, Texas, 1979–1980; Visiting critic, School of Architecture, Rice University, Houston, Texas, 1979–1981; Architectural photographer, 1979–present; President, Houston Center for Photography, Houston, Texas, 1982; Book editor, *Image*, Houston Center for Photography, Houston, Texas, 1982–1984.

Recognitions and Awards:

National Endowment for the Arts Photography Fellowship, 1973, 1980; Thomas J. Watson Traveling Fellowship in Europe,

1974; National Endowment for the Arts Photography Survey Grant, 1978; Architectural Survey of Houston, Texas Historical Commission, 1979.

Selected Individual Exhibitions:

1973—Aperture Gallery, Houston, Texas. 1978—*Signs in the Houston Landscape*, Houston Public Library, Houston, Texas; D. Clayton and Co., Houston, Texas; Blue Sky Gallery, Portland, Oregon. 1979—*La Arquitectura: Spanish Influences on Houston Architecture*, Houston Public Library, Houston, Texas; *The Tunnel System*, Houston Festival, Houston Public Library, Houston, Texas. 1980—*Our Ancestors' Graves: Houston's Historic Cemeteries*, Houston Public Library, Houston, Texas.

Selected Group Exhibitions:

1971—Latent Image Gallery, Houston, Texas. 1975—Ohio Silver Gallery, Los Angeles, California. 1978—*Southwest Works on Paper*, Dallas Museum of Art, Dallas, Texas. 1979—*Some Houston Photographers*, Alfred C. Glassell, Jr. School of Art, Museum of Fine Arts, Houston, Texas; *Anthony G. Cronin Memorial Collection*, Museum of Fine Arts, Houston, Texas. 1980—*A Second Look*, Cronin Gallery, Houston, Texas; *Texas Photographers: Four Directions*, Amarillo Art Center, Amarillo, Texas; *Fifth Anniversary Show*, Blue Sky Gallery, Portland, Oregon; *Fifth Anniversary Show*, Cronin Gallery, Houston, Texas. 1982—*First Annual Members Exhibition*, Houston Center for Photography, Houston, Texas; *Prisoners of Con-science*, Studio One, Houston, Texas; *From the Collection +*, Alfred C. Glassell, Jr. School of Art, Museum of Fine Arts, Houston, Texas. 1983—*Second Annual Members Exhibition*, Houston Center for Photography, Houston, Texas; *Messages from Earth*, Houston Center for Photography, Houston, Texas; *Houston-in-the-Round: Panoramic Photographs*, Houston Public Library, Houston, Texas. 1984—*A Personal Response: The Threat of Nuclear War*, Houston Center for Photography, Houston, Texas; *Third Annual Members Exhibition*, Houston Center for Photography, Houston, Texas; *Exposed and Developed: Photography Sponsored by the National Endowment for the Arts*, National Museum of American Art, Washington, D.C.; *Fourth Annual Photography Exhibition*, Boulevard Gallery, Houston, Texas; *The Body and Its Functions*, Nexus Gallery, Atlanta, Georgia. 1985—*National Juried Exhibition*, Houston Center for Photography, Houston, Texas; *Houston Photographers in the Museum Collection*, Museum of Fine Arts, Houston, Texas.

Books Illustrated by Hester:

Papademetriou, Peter C. *Signs in the Houston Landscape.* Houston, Texas: Houston Public Library, 1978.

Papademetriou, Peter C. *La Arquitectura: Spanish Influences on Houston Architecture.* Houston, Texas: Houston Public Library, 1979.

Milburn, Douglas. *Our Ancestors' Graves: Houston's Historic Cemeteries.* Houston, Texas: Houston Public Library, 1980.

Photographs in Published Sources:

Cook, Alison, ed. *Prisoners of Conscience*. Houston, Texas: Studio One, 1982, n.p.

"Urban Settings: A Portfolio." *Texas Architect*, vol. 32, no. 3 (May/June 1982), pp. 65–69.

Milburn, Douglas. *Houston-in-the-Round: Panoramic Photographs*. Houston, Texas: Houston Public Library, 1983.

Foresta, Merry Amanda. *Exposed and Developed: Photography Sponsored by the National Endowment for the Arts*. Washington, D.C.: Smithsonian Institution Press, 1984, pp. 7, 11, 76–77.

Collections:

Bibliothèque Nationale, Paris, France; Amon Carter Museum, Fort Worth, Texas; Houston Public Library, Houston, Texas; Museum of Fine Arts, Houston, Texas; National Museum of American Art, Washington, D.C.; Photography Collection, Harry Ransom Humanities Research Center, University of Texas, Austin, Texas; Stedelijk Museum, Amsterdam, The Netherlands.

hester

1100 Milam
Building.
Underground
cafeteria. Houston,
1984.

48

All photographs are gelatin silver prints.

RepublicBank. Loan
Department.
Houston, 1984.

Texas Commerce
Bank Tower in
United Energy Plaza.
Houston, 1984.

50

RepublicBank.
Office. Houston,
1984.

hester

Pennzoil Place.
Atrium. Houston,
1984.

52

One Shell Plaza.
Elevator lobby.
Houston, 1984.

hester

Tenneco Employee
Center. Running
track. Houston,
1984.

54

Transco Tower.
Gerald D. Hines
Interests Reception.
Houston, 1984.

hester

Interstate 610. West
Loop looking south.
Houston, 1984.

√

City Post Oak.
Dentist's Office.
Houston, 1984.

East central Texas. Since the beginning of Anglo-American settlement in Texas in the early 1800s, black Americans have played an important role in the economy and structure of society and politics in Texas. In the fifty years following the end of the Civil War, they were a pivotal force in east and east-central Texas. Although many of their descendants now live in Dallas and Houston, the roots of the contemporary black population in Texas still lie in the small towns and countryside of east Texas. The work in this book comes from a longtime interest and involvement in the life of black Texans in the rural areas of east Texas. These are the images of everyday life: Texan, North American, and black.

Frederick C. Baldwin

Place of Birth: Lausanne, Switzerland; January 25, 1929.

Residence: Houston, Texas.

Education: B.A., Columbia College, Columbia University, New York, New York, 1955.

Professional Experience:

Free-lance photographer for *Sports Illustrated* and *National Geographic*, 1958–1960; Organizer of expedition to Spitsbergen, 1960, 1962; Free-lance photographer for *Image, Mademoiselle, Town and Country, MD, Audubon*, and *Natural History*, 1962–1966; Volunteer photographer of civil rights movement for Southern Christian Leadership Conference, Georgia, 1963; Administrative director, Peace Corps, Sarawak, Borneo, 1964–1966; Free-lance photographer, Asia, and South America, 1966–1967; Free-lance photographer, New York, New York, 1967–1969; Free-lance photographer for *Newsweek, American Sportsman, Esquire, Sports Illustrated, Southern Living, Atlanta Magazine, Holiday, True, Readers Digest, Books, American Heritage, Time-Life Books, Golf, Golf Digest, Saturday Review, Nikon*, and *Travel and Leisure*, 1970–1971; Teacher and organizer of program combining photography with historical research, University of Texas, Austin, Texas, 1975; Free-lance photographer for *GEO, Town and Country, New York Times, Texas Observer*, and *Southern Exposure*, 1980; Teacher, documentary photography, University of Texas, Austin, Texas, 1981–1982; Free-lance photographer for *Southern Exposure, Historic Preservation, Town and Country, Planning, Texas Monthly, Houston, D Magazine,* and *New York Times,* 1981–1982; Photo-reporter for *Science Digest,* 1982; Director, Photojournalism Program, University of Houston, Houston, Texas, 1982–1984; Organizer of oral history project about participants in 1963 civil rights movement in Savannah, Georgia, 1983; Free-lance photographer for *New York Times,* 1983; Organizer and co-director of "Houston Foto Fest—The Month of Photography in Houston," 1984.

Recognitions and Awards:

Winedale Associate of American Studies, University of Texas, Austin, Texas, 1975–present; City of Savannah, Georgia, . . . *We Ain't What We Used To Be* . . ., 1983; Georgia Endowment for the Humanities, . . . *We Ain't What We Used To Be* . . ., 1983; Rothko Chapel Foundation, . . .*We Ain't What We Used To Be.* . ., 1983.

Selected Individual Exhibitions:

1973—Raffi Gallery, New York, New York. 1982—*Reidsville, Georgia-Saturday Night,* Houston Center for Photography, Houston, Texas. 1983—*. . . We Ain't What We Used To Be . . .,* Telfair Academy of Arts and Sciences, Savannah, Georgia; *Tiger Ridge,* Malmo Fotograficentrum, Malmo, Sweden.

Selected Group Exhibitions:

1982—*Photographs from India,* Austin Photographic Gallery, Austin, Texas. 1983—*The American Cowboys,* Library of Congress, Washington, D.C.

Photographs in Published Sources:

. . . *We Ain't What We Used To Be.* . . . Savannah, Georgia: Telfair Press, 1983.
Tiger Ridge. Amsterdam, The Netherlands: World Press Photo Awards, 1983.
"Le Texas de Wendy Watriss et Fred Baldwin." *Photo* (Paris, France), November 1983, pp. 61–68, 128.
"Texasscenter." *Bild* (Stockholm, Sweden), December 1983, pp. 4–13.
Bode, Elroy. *This Favored Place: The Texas Hill Country.* Bryan, Texas: Shearer Publishing Company, 1984.

Collections:

Amon Carter Museum, Fort Worth, Texas; Museum of Fine Arts, Houston, Texas; Harry Ransom Humanities Research Center, University of Texas, Austin, Texas.

Wendy V. Watriss

Place of Birth: San Francisco, California; February 15, 1943.

Residence: Houston, Texas.

Education: Diploma in Spanish Language and Civilization, University of Madrid, New York University Junior Year Abroad Program, Madrid, Spain, 1961; B.A., Honors Degree, Washington Square College, New York University, New York, New York, 1965.

Professional Experience:

Newspaper reporter, *St. Petersburg Times*, St. Petersburg, Florida, 1965–1967; Television producer and writer, Public Broadcast Laboratory, National Educational Television, New York, New York, 1967–1970; Radio correspondent, Westinghouse Broadcast Corporation, 1968–1969; Stringer, *Newsweek*, Eastern Europe, 1969–1970; Free-lance photojournalist and writer, 1970–present; Visiting lecturer, American Studies Program, University of Texas, Austin, Texas, 1975.

Recognitions and Awards:

Winedale Associate of American Studies, University of Texas, Austin, Texas, 1975–present; Third Prize, Magazine Published Picture Story, Pictures of the Year, School of Journalism, University of Missouri, Columbia, Missouri, 1981; Oskar Barnack Prize and News Features Award, World Press Foundation Awards, Amsterdam, The Netherlands, 1982; Silver Medal, News Features, and Award, Women's International Democratic Federation, Interpress Photo, Damascus, Syria, 1983.

Selected Group Exhibitions:

1981—*The Ties That Bind: Photographers Portray the Family*, Dougherty Cultural Arts Center, Austin, Texas. 1982—*Agent Orange*, World Press Foundation Traveling Exhibition, Amsterdam, The Netherlands. 1983—*Agent Orange: Tragic Legacy*, Houston Center for Photography, Houston, Texas. 1985—*Photojournalism in the 80's*, Hillwood Art Gallery, C. W. Post Center, Long Island University, Greenvale, New York.

Articles by Watriss:

"A Tug of War in Chad." *Christian Science Monitor*, September 10, 1970, section 2, p. 1.

"Skopje: The planners' dream city rises from earthquake rubble." *Smithsonian*, vol. 2, no. 3 (June 1971), pp. 13–19.

"It's Something Inside You." *Southern Exposure*, vol. 4, no. 4 (Winter 1976), pp. 76–81.

"Celebrating Freedom: Juneteenth." *Southern Exposure*, vol. 5, no. 1 (Spring 1977), pp. 80–87.

"T.M.P.A." *Texas Observer*, vol. 70, no. 15 (August 11, 1978), pp. 3–6, 15–17, 21.

"Seekers in the City." *Houston*, vol. 50 (February 1979), pp. 66–73.

"Comanche Peak Protestors Take Their Case to the People." *Texas Observer*, vol. 71, no. 20 (December 14, 1979), pp. 3–9.

"The Texas Nobody Knows." *Historic Preservation*, vol. 32, no. 3 (May/June 1980), pp. 20–28.

"Juneteenth." *D Magazine*, vol. 7, no. 7 (July 1980), p. 138 .

"Growing Up Southern: Roles." *Southern Exposure*, vol. 8, no. 3 (Fall 1980), pp. 88–89, 97.

"The Soul Circuit." *GEO*, vol. 2 (December 1980), p. 134 .

"Soul in the Saddle." *Houston*, vol. 52 (February 1981), pp. 36–43, 80–81.

"Agent Orange." *Texas Observer*, vol. 73, no. 19 (September 25, 1981), pp. 1, 8–13.

"Kinfolk: The People of the Ridge." *Science Digest*, vol. 90, no. 10 (October 1982), pp. 83–88, 103.

"Agent Orange." *Image*, issue 1 (March 1983), pp. 12–13.

"American Scenes." *Reflexions* (Amsterdam, The Netherlands), July/August 1983, pp. 6–7.

"Anne Tucker: Changes." *Image*, vol. 2, no. 1 (Spring 1984), pp. 11, 24.

"Eyewitness." *Image*, vol. 2, no. 1 (Spring 1984), pp. 12–15.

"Geoff Winningham: In the Beginning." *Image*, vol. 2 (Fall 1984), pp. 13–15.

Photographs in Published Sources:

Burke, Mrs. Michael. "South of the Sahara." *Signature* (July/August 1970), pp. 24–33.

Robins, Eric and Blaine Littell. *Africa: Images and Realities.* New York: Ridge Press and Praeger Publishing Company, 1971, pp. 22, 28, 62–63, 86–87, 90–91, 102–103, 106, 200.

Ranching/Mixed Agriculture Program in Niger. Washington, D.C.: Africare, 1974.

"Wendy Watriss and Fred Baldwin." *Popular Photography Annual*, 1975, pp. 96–109.

"Variations on Texas." *Texas Observer*, vol. 67, no. 24 (December 12, 1975), pp. 11–14.

Holley, Joe. "Grimes County Chronicle." *Texas Humanist*, vol. 1, no. 1 (September 1978), pp. 2–4.

"A Potpourri of Texas Women." *Texas Humanist*, vol. 2, no. 4 (December 1979), pp. 2, 4–7, back cover.

Horne, Jed. "Tracking Agent Orange." *Life*, vol. 4, no. 12 (December 1981), pp. 65–70.

"Oskar Barnack Prize, 1982: Wendy Watriss." *LEICA Fotografie* (Munich, West Germany), vol. 6 (1982), pp. 20–23.

Unger, Walter. "Das Gift . . . und Seine Opfer." *Stern* (Hamburg, West Germany), vol. 13 (April 1982), pp. 20–26.

"Min Son Ar Ocksa Ett Offer For Kriget I Vietnam." *Stopp* (Stockholm, Sweden), July 19, 1982, pp. 56–60.

Haupt, Donna. "Arson Sleuth." *Life*, vol. 6, no. 9 (September 1983), pp. 32–36, 38.

Naggar, Carole. "Le Texas de Wendy Watriss et Fred Baldwin." *Photo* (Paris, France), November 1983, pp. 61–68, 128.

"Agent Orange: A Family Album." *Mother Jones*, vol. 8, no. 9 (November 1983), pp. 40–43.

"Texasscener." *Bild* (Stockholm, Sweden), December 1983, pp. 4–13.

Bode, Elroy. *This Favored Place: The Texas Hill Country.* Bryan, Texas: Shearer Publishing Company, 1984.

"Cuba: A World Seen Through the Lens." *Houston Chronicle*, February 16, 1984, section 10, p. 3.

Cooper, Marc. "Cuba Today." *L.A. Weekly*, vol. 6 (June 1–7, 1984), cover, pp. 16–17, 19, 23.

Nicaragua: Labor, Democracy, and the Struggle for Peace. Report of the West Coast Trade Union Delegation to Nicaragua, November 1984.

Cooper, Marc. "Nicaragua Braces for Uncle Sam." *Village Voice*, December 4, 1984, pp. 25–31.

Collections:

Barker Texas History Center, University of Texas, Austin, Texas; Bibliothèque Nationale, Paris, France; Amon Carter Museum, Fort Worth, Texas; Museum of Fine Arts, Houston, Texas; Harry Ransom Humanities Research Center, University of Texas, Austin, Texas; Winedale Historical Center, University of Texas, Round Top, Texas.

Frederick Baldwin started working with Wendy Watriss in 1971. The following are activities shared by the photographers.

Grants and Awards:

Rockefeller Foundation, 1975–1979; National Endowment for the Humanities, 1975–1979; Moody Foundation, 1975–1979; Leland Fikes Foundation, 1975–1979; Sid Richardson Foundation, 1975–1979; Anchorage Foundation, 1975–1979; William Stamps Farish Fund, 1975–1979; Grant to circulate the exhibition on Grimes County, Texas, Texas Commission for the Humanities, 1977–1978; Lecomte du Nauy Award, Prize for Grimes County project, 1980; National Endowment for the Arts Survey Grant, *The Ties That Bind: Photographers Portray the Family,* under the auspices of "Women and Their Work," Austin, Texas, 1981.

Selected Individual Exhibitions:

1973—*Rural Collection I,* Portogallo and Galate Gallery, New York, New York. 1975—*A Landed Heritage,* Phillips Collection, Washington, D.C. 1976—*Four Faces of Texas,* Winedale Historical Center, University of Texas, Round Top, Texas; *Three Faces of Texas,* Telfair Academy of Arts and Sciences, Savannah, Georgia. 1977—*Photographs from Grimes County,* Rice Museum, Institute for the Arts, Rice University, Houston, Texas. 1983—*American Scenes: Images of Texas,* Canon Photo Gallery, Amsterdam, The Netherlands; *Texas Scenes,* Stockholm Fotograficentrum, Stockholm, Sweden; *Grimes County* (permanent exhibition), Grimes County Courthouse, Anderson, Texas.

Selected Group Exhibitions:

1976—*The American Family,* Philadelphia Museum of Art, Philadelphia, Pennsylvania; USIA traveling exhibit on the U.S., Eastern Europe. 1979—*Texas Photographers,* Robinson Gallery, Houston, Texas. 1980—*Four Texas Photographers,* Amarillo Art Center, Amarillo, Texas; *Mexican-Americans in the Southwest,* Dougherty Cultural Arts Center, Austin, Texas. 1983—*Texas Photographers,* Stavanger Museum, Stavanger, Norway; Juried Group Show, Museum of New Mexico, Santa Fe, New Mexico. 1984—*Rural Texas,* Department of Agriculture, Austin, Texas; *Texas,* Palais des Beaux-Arts, Charleroi, Belgium; *Black Rodeo,* Foto Biennale Enschede, Enschede, The Netherlands. 1985—*Black Texas: Scenes from Black Life in Rural East Texas,* Torino Fotografia 85, Turin, Italy; Katherine Nash Gallery, University of Minnesota, Minneapolis, Minnesota; *Houston Photographers,* Museum of Fine Arts, Houston, Texas; Houston Center for Photography, Houston, Texas.

baldwin/watriss

Leaving Home, 1984.

All photographs are gelatin silver prints.

baldwin/watriss

Wedding Reception,
1984.

baldwin/watriss

Cowboy's Prayer,
1984.

66

Visiting Deacon,
1984.

67

Kojak's Bar, 1984.

baldwin/watriss

Locker Room, 1984.

baldwin/watriss

Welcome to Miller
Time, 1984.

70

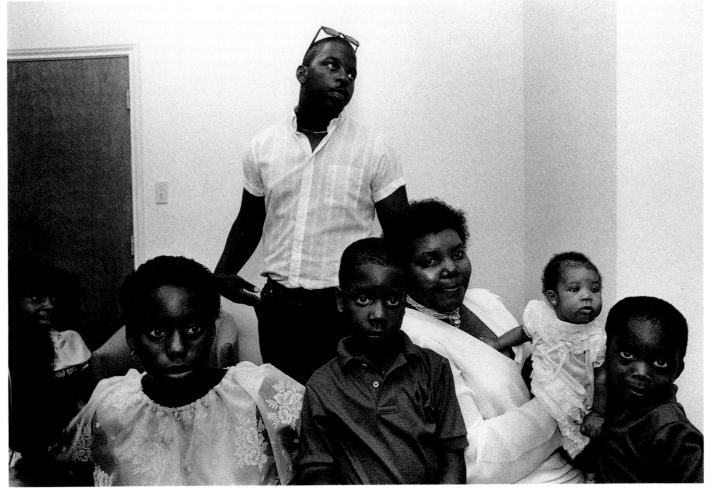

Family Reunion, 1984.

baldwin/watriss

Saturday Night,
1984.

72

baldwin/watriss

Saturday Night,
1984.

[Mary Peck photographed in the Texas Panhandle. She has chosen not to submit a statement.]

Mary Peck

Place of Birth: Minneapolis, Minnesota; July 31, 1952.

Residence: Santa Fe, New Mexico.

Education: B.F.A., Utah State University, Logan, Utah, 1974; Apprentice and assistant to Paul Caponigro, 1974–1976; Assistant to Laura Gilpin, 1977–1979.

Recognitions and Awards:

National Endowment for the Arts Photography Survey Grant, 1982.

Selected Group Exhibitions:

1975—Utah State University, Logan, Utah. 1976—*Southwest Biennial*, Museum of New Mexico, Santa Fe, New Mexico; *CS/PG*, Muckenthaler Cultural Center, Fullerton, California; Gallery f22, Santa Fe, New Mexico. 1977—*The Amarillo Competition*, Amarillo Art Center, Amarillo, Texas; *Magic Silver Show*, Murray State University, Murray, Kentucky; The Shado' Gallery, Oregon City, Oregon; *Santa Fe Armory Show*, Santa Fe, New Mexico; *National Woman's Conference Slide Exhibit*, Los Angeles, California; Gallery 244, Fort Lauderdale, Florida. 1978—*Festival IX*, Scottsdale, Arizona; *Santa Fe Armory Show*, Santa Fe, New Mexico. 1980—Shadow Catcher Gallery, Taos, New Mexico; *Photographer's Choice*, Santa Fe Festival of the Arts, Santa Fe, New Mexico; *Photo West*, Utah State University, Logan, Utah; Daniel Wolf, Inc., New York, New York. 1981—Steven Katzman Gallery, Sarasota, Florida; Studio 666, Paris, France; Daniel Wolf, Inc., New York, New York. 1982—*Earth, Clay & Stone*, Phoenix Art Museum, Phoenix, Arizona; Port Washington Library, Long Island, New York. 1983—*Contemporary Photography from the Museum Collection*, Alfred C. Glassell Jr. School of Art, Museum of Fine Arts, Houston, Texas; *Works of Winter*, Ernesto Mayans Gallery, Santa Fe, New Mexico. 1984—*Trees and Clouds*, Witkin Gal-

peck

lery, New York, New York; St. John's College, Santa Fe, New Mexico. 1985—*Southwest '85: A Fine Arts Competition*, Museum of Fine Arts, Santa Fe, New Mexico; Hoshour Gallery, Albuquerque, New Mexico; *On the Wall/Off the Wall*, Center for Contemporary Arts, Santa Fe, New Mexico; Benteler Galleries, Houston, Texas; Robischon Gallery, Denver, Colorado.

Articles and Reviews:

"Mary Peck." *New America, The Southwest: A Regional View*, vol. 3, no. 3 (Spring 1979), pp. 112–118.

Asbury, Dana. "How They Work: 3 Master Printers and Their Assistants." *Popular Photography*, vol. 89, no. 12 (December 1982), pp. 79, 82–83, 157.

Yates, Steve. "The New Mexico Survey (A Preview)." *Creative Camera*, no. 237 (September 1984), p. 1524.

Photographs in Published Sources:

"Traces from the Past." *Exploration: Annual Bulletin of the School of American Research*. Santa Fe, New Mexico: School of American Research, 1980, pp. 14–15.

Fourteen Photographers from Santa Fe. Palm Beach, Florida: Gallery Gemini, 1981, n.p.

Jackson, J. B. *The Essential Landscape: The New Mexico Photographic Survey*. Albuquerque, New Mexico: University of New Mexico Press, 1985.

Collections:

California Museum of Photography, Riverside, California; Amon Carter Museum, Fort Worth, Texas; Columbia College, Chicago, Illinois; James S. Copley Library, La Jolla, California; Krannert Art Museum, University of Illinois, Champaign, Illinois; Museum of Art, Fort Lauderdale, Florida; Museum of Fine Arts, Houston, Texas; Museum of Fine Arts, St. Petersburg, Florida; Museum of Fine Arts, Santa Fe, New Mexico; Notre Dame University, South Bend, Indiana; Photography Collection, Harry Ransom Humanities Research Center, University of Texas, Austin, Texas; Santa Barbara Museum of Art, Santa Barbara, California; University Art Gallery, New Mexico State University, Las Cruces, New Mexico.

peck

Abandoned
homesite, Rita
Blanca Grasslands,
Texas, 1984.

All photographs are gelatin silver prints.

77

Wheatfield,
Happy, Texas, 1984.

peck

peck

Cotton trailers,
Easter, Texas, 1984.

peck

Freight train, near
Amarillo, Texas,
1984.

peck

Big top,
Dalhart, Texas, 1984.

Hippopotamu,
Dalhart, Texas, 1984.

82

Near Lesley, Texas,
1984.

peck

peck

Near
Umbarger, Texas,
1984.

peck

Gibson's fire,
Childress, Texas,
1984.

85

Mitchell 450,
Spearman, Texas,
1984.

michael allen murphy

My project was to photograph a group of people in Texas who could be termed "movers and shapers" of policy, business, and industry; people who have made outstanding contributions in their particular field. The idea was to photograph each individual in a setting that would reveal something of the particular accomplishments he or she had made and at the same time provide a good portrait of the subject.

I began the task in earnest in early July 1984 by compiling a list of twenty-seven persons whom I then wrote and requested permission to photograph. I conferred with Scott Bennett, editor of *Texas Business* magazine, for his ideas of people whom I might include.

Each person was sent a cover letter introducing my role in the project, a brochure describing the project, and a letter requesting permission for a photographic appointment. I requested time for a portrait from most potential subjects, but of a few I also requested that I be allowed to follow them for a day. This was in hopes of getting a more candid look at the individual.

My thinking was that if I could get a fifty percent response, I would have fifteen portraits, and the best ten could be included in the exhibition and book. After a great deal of work, including many phone calls attempting to penetrate the protective layers surrounding most of the subjects, I was able to obtain fourteen portraits.

The bulk of the photography was done in August and early September 1984. I was pleased for the most part with the sessions I had, but disappointed that some of the individuals I had really hoped to photograph were unable to participate.

The youngest individual I photographed was Dr. Sally Ride, America's first woman in space. The oldest, at age eighty-nine, was W. A. "Monty" Moncrief, a renowned Texas oilman. The busiest individual was Dr. Michael DeBakey, who at seventy-six works at a pace that would frazzle most people one-third his age. All were quite receptive to the idea of the project and felt it was an honor to be included. Time actually spent photographing the individuals ranged from ten minutes to half a day. In many cases I would be completely ready to go, the subject would arrive, and the session would be over in a very short time.

The opportunity to meet and photograph each person was something that could have happened only through a project of this nature, and I feel privileged to have been part of such an ambitious project. I just hope that, in future years when this work is studied, those viewing it will realize that the ten individuals included are but a small percentage of a very large group collectively called "movers and shapers."

Michael Allen Murphy

Place of Birth: Houston, Texas; December 1, 1952.

Residence: Dripping Springs, Texas.

Education: B.J., University of Texas, Austin, Texas, 1976; M.A., University of Texas, Austin, Texas, 1982.

Professional Experience:

Photojournalist, *Daily Texan*, University of Texas, Austin, Texas, 1976; Teaching assistant, University of Texas, Austin, Texas, 1976–1978; Photojournalist, *Dallas Morning News*, 1978; Photojournalist, *Houston Chronicle*, 1979; Photojournalist, Texas Tourist Development Agency, Austin, Texas, 1979–1983; Lecturer, University of Texas, Austin, Texas, 1982–1984; Free-lance photographer, 1983–present.

Selected Group Exhibitions:

1979—*The Texas Prison Rodeo*, Laguna Gloria at First Federal, Austin, Texas.

Collections:

Amon Carter Museum, Fort Worth, Texas; Museum of Fine Arts, Houston, Texas; Photography Collection, Harry Ransom Humanities Research Center, University of Texas, Austin, Texas.

Houston Mayor
Katherine J.
Whitmire in her
office, 1984.

All photographs are gelatin silver prints.

murphy

Arthur Temple,
lumber magnate, in
Lufkin, 1984.

Herbert Kelleher,
Chief of Southwest
Airlines, at Love
Field in Dallas,
1984.

Richard and Stanley
Marcus in the
Oriental Gallery at
Neiman-Marcus
(Downtown) Dallas,
1984.

murphy

T. Boone Pickens,
Chief of Mesa
Petroleum, near his
2-B ranch northeast
of Amarillo, 1984.

murphy

Dr. Michael
DeBakey, renowned
surgeon, in his
office, Houston,
1984.

94

Ben Love, banker,
Texas Commerce
Bank, Houston,
1984.

murphy

W. A. "Monty"
Moncrief, son W. A.
"Tex" Moncrief, Jr.,
and grandsons
Richard W. Moncrief
and Charles B.
Moncrief at the
Moncrief Building,
Fort Worth, 1984.

Lieutenant Governor
William P. Hobby in
the Senate
Chambers, Austin,
1984.

murphy

Dr. Sally Ride in the
shuttle trainer,
NASA, 1984.

98

carol cohen burton

Texas in the 1980s is becoming a network of large cities. Prairies turn overnight into shopping centers. Icons of growth gleam all around us. My goal was to photograph a Texas brushed in by growth and change—to construct photographic "canvases" by playing on the tension between the sensuality of color and the "baseness" of commonly found objects.

My photographs are taken from the highways, farm and ranch roads, and city streets. They show a Texas landscape seen constantly, but show it, a common view, uncommonly. My vantage point emphasizes transportation systems, the relationship between town and country as connected by our road systems, the construction rampant in both urban and rural areas of Texas.

Symbols of the land in change, the economy in growth are everywhere in Texas. I chose to concentrate within boundaries set by interstate highways 35, 30, 45, and 10. This was due to the symbolic nature of the shape formed by the connecting highways, to the central location within the giant state, and to the fact that the area was most accessible to me from my Austin home base. These boundaries drew, broadly, a "cone"—like a ubiquitous orange highway marker—between the major cities of Austin, Fort Worth, Dallas, Houston, and San Antonio. I photographed large cities, small towns, and the rural "in between."

Next, I chose to focus on forms used in construction—barriers, banners, arrows, flags, bright orange cones—forms immediately recognizable to travelers in our times . . . forms signaling growth and change. My objective was to allow these "things" to claim the strange and magical quality that is theirs. Shown as sculptural objects, "things" become extraordinary creatures with life and beauty and a tug on our souls.

Finally, I chose especially to note the incredible sweep of land, the expanse of sky, the quality of light in the Texas landscape—whether town or country. These "incidentals" summon the best in our human spirits and allow the symbols and patterns of our times a sense of magic and grace.

Carol Cohen Burton

Place of Birth: Cleburne, Texas; January 17, 1945.

Residence: Austin, Texas.

Education: B.F.A., with honors, University of Texas, Austin, Texas, 1967; Instituto Allende, San Miguel de Allende, Mexico, Summer, 1968.

Professional Experience:

Free-lance photographer and restoration color consultant, 1979–present; Instructor of photography, St. Stephen's Episcopal School, Austin, Texas, 1980–present.

Recognitions and Awards:

H.E.W. Title V Fellowship Recipient, 1967–1969.

Selected Individual Exhibitions:

1981 Fourth Street Photo Gallery, New York, New York. 1983—Accent Gallery, Austin, Texas; *Color by Carol Cohen*, University of Texas Health Science Center, San Antonio, Texas.

Selected Group Exhibitions:

1968—*Eight Students of Russell Lee*, Texas Lutheran College, Seguin, Texas. 1979—*Amarillo Competition*, Amarillo Art Center, Amarillo, Texas. 1983—*Austin Photographic Co-Op Group Exhibit*, Gallery 104, Austin, Texas; *Live and in Color from Austin, Texas: Color Photos by Seven*, PhotoWork Gallery, Austin, Texas. 1984—*Selected Portfolios: 1984 Texas Photographic Society Members Exhibition*, PhotoWork Gallery, Austin, Texas; *Sixth Annual Austin Contemporary Art Exhibition*, Dougherty Arts Center, Austin, Texas.

Photographs in Published Sources:

University of Texas Fall and Winter Books Catalog. Austin: University of Texas Press, 1983, cover.

Collections:

Amon Carter Museum, Fort Worth, Texas; Helmut Gernsheim Collection, Lugano, Switzerland; Museum of Fine Arts, Houston, Texas; Photography Collection, Harry Ransom Humanities Research Center, University of Texas, Austin, Texas.

cohen burton

Cowtown.
Fort Worth,
July 6, 1984.

101

cohen burton

Industrial Yellow.
Dallas, July 7, 1984.

cohen burton

Country Barrier.
East of Montgomery,
August 5, 1984.

cohen burton

Truck Transport.
Fort Worth,
July 6, 1984.

104

OWN A
SIGN LIKE
THIS
$35.00
PER MONTH
CONROE 756-6408 TEXAS
TEXAS SIGN
BUILDERS

cohen burton

Own a Sign. Conroe,
August 4, 1984.

cohen burton

Corrugation with
Banner. Austin,
May 9, 1984.

cohen burton

Town and Country
Mall. Temple,
July 5, 1984.

107

cohen burton

Barrier Highway.
Austin,
May 24, 1984.

108

cohen burton

Rural Road. West of
Ennis, July 8, 1984.

cohen burton

Prairie City. Dallas,
July 7, 1984.

rick williams

Albany, Texas, is a town of approximately 2,500 people and is located on the northeast border of the oil-rich Permian Basin, thirty miles north of Abilene and two hundred miles west of Fort Worth. If Fort Worth is the "Gateway to the West," Albany is the first fork in the road beyond that gateway. It is a stepping-off point into a land of history, legend, and myth, a land of grass and mesquite that is flat to the eye from the highway but laced with deep gullies and canyons from horseback.

This is a land where Watt Matthews' grandparents and their pioneer contemporaries settled, fought Indians, cleared land, and shaped huge cattle ranches out of wilderness. It is a land where the peace was once won from a transient band of Fort Griffin traders and soldiers with taut vigilante ropes and smoking six-guns. From the beginning of the white man's siege in the early 1800s Albany was the reality that shaped the myths of the pioneer, the rancher, the cowboy, and the desperado and more recently the evolving myths of the roughneck, driller, and Texas oil man.

While Albany is representative of many historical, rural, agricultural areas in Texas, both in its history and in its more contemporary trends, it is also unique and special. This uniqueness centers around the way that its people have so artistically and successfully merged a traditional ranching community with a more urban oil and gas community since 1920. They have managed to utilize the resources of both communities to develop a culture that is prosperous, vibrant, sophisticated, and progressive while continuing to embrace traditional rural values and to foster both the reality and the myth of the historical and cultural flavor of the area.

111

During the past four years I have spent more than twelve months photographing the people of Albany, Texas, and documenting their lifestyles, traditions and interrelationships.

My interaction with these people through photography, interviews, research, social events, and simply living among them has stimulated me to think about the rural traditions and myths that are expressed in their lifestyles. In doing so I have come to believe that in the myths and traditions expressed in the lifestyles of the people of rural communities we have a direct link with our heritage, our physical roots, and our spirit as a people. Therefore, I also believe that as these rural people change and as their lifestyles change and adapt to the influences of a rapidly changing, highly urbanized society, the documentation of their lifestyles becomes both culturally and historically significant to us all.

The ten photographs reproduced here represent my most recent work in Albany and are indicative of my efforts to explore a broader spectrum of the Albany socialscape than I did in my earlier work, which was limited primarily to ranch life. While this work includes oil field workers, executives, grocery clerks, and social events, the order in which they are presented is designed to provide some continuity and to reveal similarities, contrasts, and relationships that I see among the various people and groups.

Rick Williams

Place of Birth: Houston, Texas; October 15, 1946.

Residence: Austin, Texas.

Education: B.J., University of Texas, Austin, Texas, 1970.

Professional Experience:

Director of advertising and public relations, Sea-Arama Marineworld, Galveston, Texas, 1970–1971; Advertising account executive, Alert Advertising Agency, Galveston, Texas, 1972–1973; Free-lance photographer, 1973–present; Consultant for electronic media relations in the southwest, Dow Chemical—USA, Houston, Texas, 1974–1976; Director of student activities and student union, Chairman of publications board, and Advisor to student publications, St. Edward's University, Austin, Texas, 1976–1980; Adjunct instructor of photography, St. Edward's University, Austin, Texas, 1977–1980.

Recognitions and Awards:

Grant for research and preparation of a proposal to develop a degree program in photocommunications, St. Edward's University, Austin, Texas, 1978; Grant to develop photocommunication degree program including curriculum design, equipment purchase and installation, and facility design and construction, St. Edward's University, Austin, Texas, 1980; First Place, real estate, *Houston Art Director's Club Show*, Houston, Texas, 1980; Local, regional, and national Addy Awards, *Desperado Boots*, 1980; Commission from Old Jail Foundation, *The Women of Albany*, Albany, Texas, 1981; Best black and white of show purchase, *Focus on Oil*, Permian Basin Petroleum Museum, Midland, Texas, 1981; Jurors' Purchase Award, *Sixteenth Annual Southwest Area Art Show*, Museum of the Southwest, Midland, Texas, 1982; Jurors' Purchase Award, *Spring Exhibition*, Austin Contemporary Visual Arts Association, Austin, Texas, 1984; Tracor Publications brochure, *International Competition Exhibition*, Society of Typographic Artists, Chicago, Illinois, 1984; Publication Award, *Print Magazine*, 1984.

Selected Individual Exhibitions:

1981—*Selected Works*, St. Edward's University Gallery, Austin, Texas. 1982—*Albany*, Old Jail Foundation, Albany, Texas. 1984—*Common Ground*, Texas Arts Alliance Gallery, Abilene, Texas.

Selected Group Exhibitions:

1969—Mental Health Mental Retardation Traveling Exhibit, Texas. 1972—*Galveston Photographers*, Galveston Center on the Strand, Galveston, Texas. 1980—*1980 Book of Days*, Austin, Texas. 1981—*Fifteenth Annual Southwest Area Art Show*, Museum of the Southwest, Midland, Texas; *Focus on Oil*, Per-

mian Basin Petroleum Museum, Midland, Texas. 1983—*Seventeenth Annual Southwest Area Art Show*, Museum of the Southwest, Midland, Texas; *Texas Only*, Texas Fine Arts Association, Austin, Texas; *Citation Exhibition*, Texas Fine Arts Association, Austin, Texas; *Members' Juried Exhibition*, Texas Photographic Society, PhotoWork Gallery, Austin, Texas. 1984—*Spring Exhibition*, Austin Contemporary Visual Arts Association, Austin, Texas; *Reflections*, Museum of the Southwest, Midland, Texas; *Members' Juried Exhibition*, Texas Photographic Society, PhotoWork Gallery, Austin, Texas.

Photographs in Published Sources:

Green, Bob. *The Women of Albany*. Albany, Texas: Old Jail Foundation, 1985. (Portfolio)

Collections:

Amon Carter Museum, Fort Worth, Texas; Museum of Fine Arts, Houston, Texas; Museum of the Southwest, Midland, Texas; Old Jail Foundation Museum, Albany, Texas; Permian Basin Petroleum Museum, Midland, Texas; Photography Collection, Harry Ransom Humanities Research Center, University of Texas, Austin, Texas.

williams

Derrick Hand
Stacking Pipe, Jones
Rig #51, Near
Albany, Texas,
July 1984.

114   *All photographs are gelatin silver prints.*

Roy Hurd Moore
Cleaning Stable,
Davis Ranch,
Merkel, Texas,
July 1984.

A.V. Jones, Jones Oil
Company,
Albany, Texas,
June 1984.

Bob Green, Green
Ranch,
Albany, Texas,
June 1984.

117

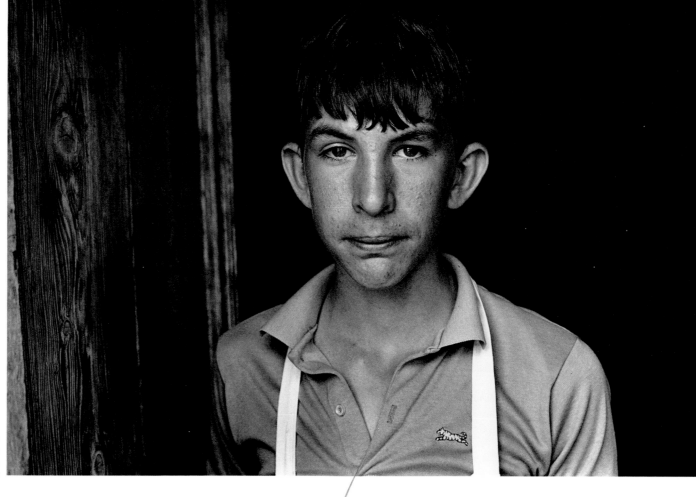

williams

Jerry Lee Arnold,
Clerk, City Grocery,
Albany, Texas,
June 1984.

118

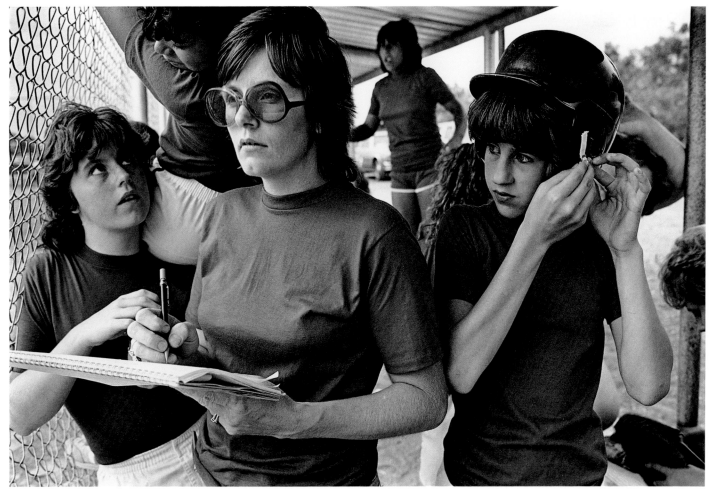

Girls' Softball Game,
Albany, Texas,
June 1984.

williams

Saddle Blanket
and Harness,
Green Ranch,
Albany, Texas,
June 1984.

120

williams

Bennie Peacock,
Foreman,
Green Ranch,
Albany, Texas,
June 1984.

williams

Rounding Up Strays,
Matador, Texas,
November 1982.

122

williams

Branding and
Cutting,
Matador, Texas,
April 1983.

peter helms feresten

For several years I have enjoyed the unparalleled privilege and good fortune to practice my craft in Fort Worth's black community. Ignored by the white mainstream that seems determined to promote a western middle-class illusion, black neighborhoods have developed their own institutions reflecting a southern working-class reality.

Churches, fraternal organizations, and social, charity, and art clubs reflect and sometimes parody similar white institutions while they focus on and express a deeper culture. I speak of a culture to which all participants contribute, one that tolerates no mere spectators. I speak of a culture that has sustained an oppressed people through prolonged hardship.

As opportunities gradually open to Texas' black citizens during a period of economic growth, institutions that were spawned in poverty and isola-

tion threaten to give way to the culture of commerce, to the homogenized soup of generic America. We all sacrifice a great deal when we abandon the values that sustained our parents in exchange for the illusion of culture presented by T.V. sitcoms. As we wall our suburbs and ma(u)ll our cities, we remove ourselves from human scale. As we concentrate by class we destroy the vertically integrated urban village. Our institutions cease to represent a cross section of our society. Our culture ceases to reflect the aspirations of an entire people.

The black neighborhoods of Fort Worth are urban villages, America's true small towns. The culture of their most humble institutions is poetic and runs deep. As mainstream America aspires to Madison Avenue's standards, and as "culture" is perverted to mean the consumption of Europe's dead past, my mind wanders to the south side of town. The mean-

125

ing of culture is clear where the music is more moving, the food is spicier, and voices speak the language of the heart.

Peter Helms Feresten

Place of Birth: Newport, Rhode Island; June 15, 1945.

Residence: Fort Worth, Texas.

Education: Studied Sociology at Columbia University, New York, New York, 1963–1967; B.F.A., Rhode Island School of Design, Providence, Rhode Island, 1972; M.F.A., Rhode Island School of Design, Providence, Rhode Island, 1974.

Professional Experience:

Assistant professor of photography, Tarrant County Junior College, Hurst, Texas, 1975–present; Workshop instructor, *The City Building Project*, Fort Worth Art Museum, Fort Worth, Texas, 1976; Director of exhibition, *Light on Fort Worth*, Elmwood Foundation for the Arts and Humanities, Fort Worth, Texas, 1980; Assembled and prepared exhibit, *American Crisis: Photographs from Magnum Photos, Inc.*, University of Texas Health Science Center, San Antonio, Texas, 1980.

Recognitions and Awards:

Award, *Southwest Artists' Annual*, Fort Worth Art Museum, Fort Worth, Texas, 1976; General Media Award, Mayfest Art Awards, Fort Worth, Texas, 1978; Purchase Award, Bellevue Art Museum, Bellevue, Washington, 1979; Awards, Mule Alley Galleries, Fort Worth, Texas, 1981; Award, *Saint John's Annual Religious Art Festival*, Sacramento, California, 1981; First Prize, Mayfest Art Awards, Fort Worth, Texas, 1983; Juror's Award, *Art in the Metroplex*, Texas Christian University, Fort Worth, Texas, 1983, 1984.

Selected Individual Exhibitions:

1975—Woods-Gerry Gallery, Rhode Island School of Design, Providence, Rhode Island. 1978—Afterimage Gallery, Dallas, Texas; D. W. Gallery, Dallas, Texas. 1979—Art Department, Texas Wesleyan College, Fort Worth, Texas. 1980—Rice Media Center, Rice University, Houston, Texas; Colorado Mountain College, Breckenridge, Colorado. 1982—*Peter Feresten: Photographs and Soundpiece*, Department of Art, Texas Woman's University, Denton, Texas.

Selected Group Exhibitions:

1975—*Photography as a Fine Art*, University of Florida, Gainesville, Florida. 1976—*Southwest Artists' Annual*, Fort Worth Art Museum, Fort Worth, Texas. 1977—*Plastic Camera Show*, Dallas New Arts Festival, Macy Gallery, Dallas, Texas; *Three Photographers*, University of Illinois, Champaign, Illinois; *Southwest Artists' Annual*, Fort Worth Art Museum, Fort Worth, Texas. 1978—*Big Name Invitational*, 500 X Gallery, Dallas, Texas; *Plastic Camera Photographs*, Meadows School of the Arts, Southern Methodist University, Dallas, Texas.

1979—*Peter Feresten: Photographs, and John Moore: Drawings*, Hall of State, Fair Park, Dallas, Texas; *Alumni Exhibition*, Rhode Island School of Design, Providence, Rhode Island; *American Vision*, New York University, New York, New York; *Photoworks 79*, Bellevue Art Museum, Bellevue, Washington; Zollar Art Gallery, Pennsylvania State University, College Station, Pennsylvania; *Fish*, Boston College, Boston, Massachusetts. 1980—*Personal and Public Documents*, Massachusetts Institute of Technology, Cambridge, Massachusetts; *Emerging Texas Photographers*, Laguna Gloria Art Museum, Austin, Texas; *Exposure*, Museum of Science and History, Fort Worth, Texas; *The Collection Exhibition*, Hills Gallery, Denver, Colorado; *Selected Works of Dallas Photographers*, Allen Street Gallery, Dallas, Texas. 1981—*Works on Paper*, Mule Alley Galleries, Fort Worth, Texas; Saint John's Annual Religious Art Festival, Saint John's Lutheran Church, Sacramento, California. 1982—*Aural Sets*, 500 X Gallery, Dallas, Texas; *Between Twelve and Twenty*, Loomis Chaffee School, Windsor, Connecticut; *Five Years at the Creative Photography Gallery*, Massachusetts Institute of Technology, Cambridge, Massachusetts. 1983—*Photography Invitational*, Austin College, Sherman, Texas; *The Artist's Eye*, Kimbell Art Museum, Fort Worth, Texas; *Recent Figurative Work*, 500 X Gallery, Dallas, Texas; *Three Exceptional Photographers*, Afterimage Gallery, Dallas, Texas; *Art in the Metroplex*, Texas Christian University, Fort Worth, Texas; *Three Texas Photographers*, Hills Gallery, Denver, Colorado. 1984—*Art in the Metroplex*, Texas Christian University, Fort Worth, Texas; *Dwellings*, Commu-nity College of Morris City, Morris City, New Jersey; *Images*, Texas Christian University, Fort Worth, Texas; *Current Works*, Morgan Gallery, Kansas City, Missouri; *Current Works*, Edwynn Houk Gallery, Chicago, Illinois; *Allen Street Gallery Retrospective*, Allen Street Gallery, Dallas, Texas.

Articles by Feresten:

"Light on Fort Worth." *Dallas Arts Review*, vol. 1, no. 2 (September 1979), pp. 4–5.

Articles and Reviews:

Dillon, David. "The Solitary Eye." *D Magazine*, vol. 5, no. 6 (June 1978), pp. 91–95.

Park, Glenna. "Piano Grins and Amens." *Texas Jazz*, vol. 2, no. 11 (November 1978), p. 1.

Carrora, Francine. "Gallery." *Dallas Photo*, vol. 1, no. 8 (November 1978), pp. 22–24.

Kutner, Janet. "Texas Photographer Heads Local Exhibitions." *Dallas Morning News*, November 1, 1978.

Holsomback, Barbara. "Photographer Leaves Legacy." *Fort Worth Star-Telegram*, northeast edition, November 1–2, 1978.

Seiberling, Christopher. "Testimony of the Participant—Mystique of the Witness." *Views: A New England Journal of Photography*, vol. 1, no. 3 (Spring 1980), p. 27.

Lowe, Ron. "Camera Captures Black Religious Ritual." *Fort Worth Star-Telegram*, July 25, 1982, pp. 1E, 5E.

Fox, Kevin. "Figuring It Out." *Dallas Downtown News* (May

30–June 5, 1983).

Kutner, Janet. "500 X Gallery Spotlights New Talent." *Dallas Morning News*, June 7, 1983.

Photographs in Published Sources:

Holmes, Jon. "Texas: An Example." *Camera*, vol. 56, no. 8 (August 1977), pp. 5–6.

Park, Glenna. "Peter Feresten and Charlie DeBus." *Artweek*, vol. 9, no. 8 (February 25, 1978), p. 12.

Artweek, vol. 9, no. 37 (November 4, 1978), pp. 14.

Harris, Paul Rogers. *Emerging Texas Photographers*. Austin, Texas: Laguna Gloria Art Museum, 1980, pp. 22–23, 32.

Kalil, Susie. "Texas Portfolio." *Artweek*, vol. 11, no. 41 (December 6, 1980), p. 1.

Embry, Charles R., ed. *Sulphur River Poetry Review*, vol. 3, no. 2, front cover, back cover, pp. 15–18.

Hoffman, Fred. "A Portfolio of Texas Photography." *Arts and Architecture*, vol. 1, no. 2 (Winter 1981), p. 38.

Rabetz, Walter, ed. *Between Twelve and Twenty: A Photographic Exploration of Young People Today*. Windsor, Connecticut: Loomis Chaffee School, 1982, p. 77.

Holmes, Jon. *Texas: A Self Portrait*. New York: Harry N. Abrams, 1983, pp. 216–217, 221, 229–230.

Lowe, Ron. "Fort Worth." *Artspace*, vol. 7, no. 2 (Spring 1983), p. 28.

Collections:

Bellevue Art Museum, Bellevue, Washington; Amon Carter Museum, Fort Worth, Texas; Dallas Museum of Art, Dallas, Texas; Museum of Fine Arts, Houston, Texas; Photography Collection, Harry Ransom Humanities Research Center, University of Texas, Austin, Texas.

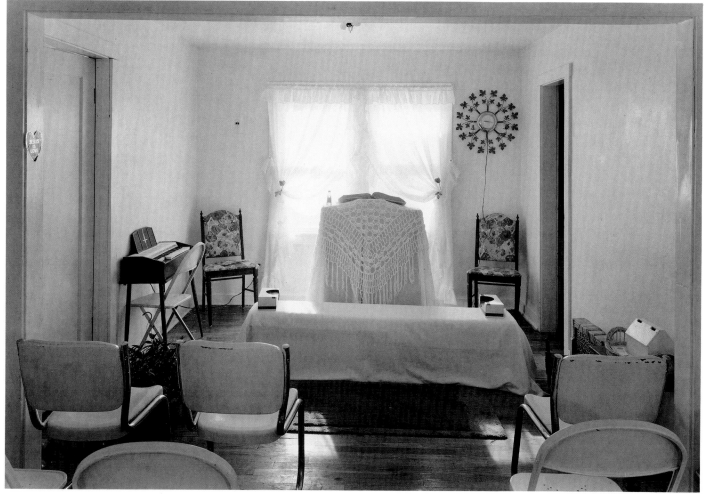

feresten

The Ark of God.
Fort Worth, 1983.

Evangelist Scott.
Fort Worth, 1983.

feresten

Bright Glory Baptist
Church.
Fort Worth, 1983.

131

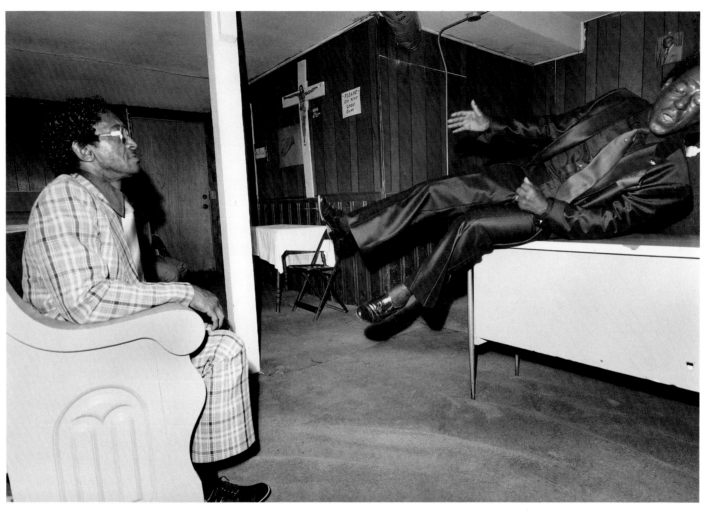

Abraham's Sacrifice.
Calumet Baptist
Church.
Fort Worth, 1984.

feresten

Love Temple, New
Born Holiness
Church.
Fort Worth, 1983.

feresten

Master Masons,
Prince Hall Grand
Lodge. Fort Worth,
1984.

134

Grand High Court,
Heroines of Jericho,
Prince Hall Grand
Lodge. Fort Worth,
1984.

feresten

Most Worshipful
Grand Master,
Rueben G. White;
Installation of
Officers, Prince Hall
Grand Lodge.
Fort Worth, 1984.

136

feresten

Masonic Mosque,
Prince Hall
Affiliation, Free and
Accepted Masons,
Jurisdiction of Texas;
East 1st Street.
Fort Worth, 1984.

137

feresten

Miss Juneteenth,
Sycamore Park.
Fort Worth, 1984.

stuart d. klipper

In the past couple of years I have made two forays into Texas to make photographs. The most recent of these was made at the request of the Texas Historical Foundation for its sesquicentennial project. The trip resulted in a body of work from which the images in this book were selected. These photographs, as well as everything else I have photographed in Texas, have helped to expand a large and continually growing body of my work that I call "The World in a Few States." This is a varied and amorphous agglomeration of photographs that I have made over the past five years while traveling in different regions of the United States.

"The World in a Few States" is an intentional double *entendre*. I felt that it might indicate that this work is filled with intentional ambiguities; that, in this sort of photography, there is more going on than what happens when the image initially meets the eye. Photography can be far more reflective and contemplative than most people might suppose. For me photography is as much a way of making philosophical inquiry as it is a way of engaging in a visual art. These activities complement each other. And both require an equally passionate devotion.

My art then is not directly about describing and documenting per se. These are indeed inherent to photography's processes but its unerring verisimilitude is also a wonderful "tool" to approach the metaphor—the poetic. This is what I seem to be particularly concerned with. The pictures are not immediately about the depicted places and situations. They are more akin to something like being about the "about-ness" of what in the world has been so clearly recorded by the camera.

My preoccupations seem to dwell on the elemental—the "is-ness" of the world. I make journeys through it in a kaleidoscope of shifting frames of reference. Intuition and intellect interplay. I visit parts of the United States having some general familiarity about them (I do a fair amount of homework beforehand) but nevertheless ceaselessly continue to explore. What is familiar to us can often be the most enigmatic. The familiar is always being redefined by new discoveries and revelations. This is what happens as I wander around. In exploring I half look for places and phenomena I suspect might be there and half look with no notion whatsoever about what I might be looking for except the prospect of discovery. I came to Texas, then, not only with a camera and loads of film but also with these sorts of concerns and predispositions. My need to counterpoint two polarities: this working with photography in broad philosophical terms about how the world is for us and looking at it "geographically" too. I also carry my idiosyncratic inventory of what I like to look at, what especially catches my attention. What might best define a region. How what I look at is seen by the people who live there; how I can temper my views with their idealizations and vernacular. I discover and distill certain elements of a region's natural, cultural, and

social history. I work in a web of similarities and connections between what I find where I am and what I have seen elsewhere.

An important item in my inventory: industry— the geometries and topography of technology. In Texas, petrochemical complexes. These are places essential to Texas and essentially Texan. From my earlier experiences, I knew that these expanses of industrial terrain would have to be part of what I was crystallizing as Texas' heraldry.

On my previous visit the petrochemical plants were inaccessible. Then I was at best only able to see them from outside a fence. Now I had access. The project was supported by Conoco, Inc. I thought I might now engineer entrance; get at its innards. I did. I was glad and grateful for the opportunity.

I made a group of photographs that place one in the interior of an industrial "organism"; it is viscera. The photographs in turn connote something more fundamental about being in the inside, and about being in the midst of productive activity.

I feel the photographs are also glimpses of mysterious places. I know not everyone may be as intrigued as I am as to what the guts of a petrochemical plant look and seem like, but all people encounter situations that they are exterior to. It is inherently human to be curious about what is going on just beyond one's ken.

Kin as well as ken. And imprinting, homage, and pilgrimage. When I was very young I lived in Texas for about a year. It was wartime and my dad's company needed him to go work in the office of one of their petrochemical plants in Amarillo. Life there was very different from what we were used to in New York City (being around only three or four years old, I couldn't have been used to very much yet).

I left with experiences and impressions that stayed with me throughout the years. Stories of our stay entered into the family's folklore; I still have snapshots of me dressed as a cowboy, of Mom and Dad young with their first car. Texas early formed part of me. Though it took me a long time to get back and look around, I am happy I did.

Stuart D. Klipper

Place of Birth: The Bronx, New York; August 27, 1941.

Residence: Minneapolis, Minnesota.

Education: B.A., University of Michigan, Ann Arbor, Michigan, 1962.

Professional Experience:

Camera and production work, University of Michigan T.V. Center, 1960–1964; Teaching assistant, College of Architecture and Design, University of Michigan, Ann Arbor, Michigan, 1964; Camera and editing for educational film production companies, New York, New York, 1966–1968; Still and film photography, interviewing and editing for BBC production, *D. H. Lawrence in New Mexico*, 1969; Instructor of photography, Minneapolis College of Art and Design, Minneapolis, Minnesota, 1970, 1972, 1974; Photographer for Siah Armajani, art work and structures, 1971–1978; Photographer, Sierra Club Wilderness Survey of projected Voyageurs National Park, 1972; Visiting artist, Jamestown College, Jamestown, North Dakota, 1972; Instructor of photography and assistant professor, University of Minnesota, Studio Arts Department, Extension Division and Graduate School, Minneapolis, Minnesota, 1975–1976; Instructor of photography, Blake School, Minneapolis, Minnesota, 1975–1976; Visiting artist, Minneapolis College of Art and Design, Minneapolis, Minnesota, 1975–1976; Workshop and seminar lecturer and instructor, Lightworks Photography Workshops, Minneapolis, Minnesota, 1977; Visiting artist, Minnetonka Art Center, Minnetonka, Minnesota, 1977; Visiting artist, Sun Foundation, Peoria, Illinois, 1977; Visiting artist, Art Institute of Chicago School, Chicago, Illinois, 1977; Research and production for *Press Photography: Minnesota since 1930*, Walker Art Center, Minneapolis, Minnesota, 1977–1978; Workshop instructor, Walker Art Center, Minneapolis, Minnesota, 1978; Visiting artist, University of Wisconsin, Stevens Point, Wisconsin, 1978; Visiting artist, Walker Art Center, Minneapolis, Minnesota, 1978; Visiting artist, Michigan Technical University, Houghton, Michigan, 1978; Guest curator, *Seven Photographers*, Macalester College Gallery, St. Paul, Minnesota, 1978; Visiting professor, Colorado College, Colorado Springs, Colorado, 1978–1980, 1984; Visiting artist, Carleton College, Northfield, Minnesota, 1980; Visiting professor, School of Art, University of Michigan, Ann Arbor, Michigan, 1984.

Recognitions and Awards:

Minnesota State Arts Council Grant to Visual Artists, 1974–1975; Cash Award, *Photography of St. Paul*, Minnesota Museum of Art, St. Paul, Minnesota, 1976; Minnesota State Arts Board Technical Assistance Grant, 1976–1977; National Endowment for the Arts Photography Survey Grant, 1976–1977; National Endowment for the Arts Photographers Fellowship, 1979–1980; Guggenheim Foundation Fellowship, 1979–1980; Bush Foundation Visual Artists Fellowship, St. Paul, Minnesota, 1980–1981; Commission from the Art Institute of Chicago, Chicago, Illinois, *Anasazi Places*, 1981; Commission from Cray Research, Inc., Minneapolis, Minnesota, *The Cray 1 Computer*, 1981; Commission from the First Bank Systems, Minneapolis, Minnesota, *The World in a Few States*, 1981; SECCA Awards in the Visual Arts Fellowship Nominee, 1981, 1982; Bronze Medal, *Covek i more*, International Triennial Exhibition, Zadar, Yugoslavia, 1982; Commission from Republic-Bank, Houston, Texas, *Texas Photographs*, 1983; McKnight Foundation/F.I.T.C. Fellowship, St. Paul, Minnesota, 1984; Commission from the St. Paul Companies, 1984; Commission from the state of Minnesota, 1985.

Selected Individual Exhibitions:

1964—Gallery East, Detroit, Michigan. 1972—Ragaust Gallery, Jamestown, North Dakota; Minneapolis Institute of Arts, Minneapolis, Minnesota. 1973—Unitarian Center Gallery, Minneapolis, Minnesota; JCC Gallery, Minneapolis, Minnesota. 1974—Suzanne Kohn Gallery, St. Paul, Minnesota. 1975—O.K. Harris Works of Art, New York, New York. 1976—Peter M. David Gallery, Minneapolis, Minnesota. 1978—Peter M. David Gallery, Minneapolis, Minnesota; Walker Art Center, Minneapolis, Minnesota. 1979—Theodore Lyman Wright Art Center, Beloit College, Beloit, Wisconsin; Kenyon Gallery, Chicago, Illinois; *Duluth Pictures from the Minnesota Survey*, Tweed Museum of Art, Duluth, Minnesota; *Parts of Miami Beach*, Midland Bank: Arts and Business Program, Minneapolis, Minnesota. 1980—*Three Photographic Groups*, Landmark Center, Minnesota Museum of Art, St. Paul, Minnesota; *Recent Work*, Kenyon Gallery, Chicago, Illinois; *Transitional/ Peripheral Areas*, Carleton College, Northfield, Minnesota; *Black and White Photographs: 1974–1977*, Film in the Cities Gallery, St. Paul, Minnesota. 1982—*Cosas Patagonicas*, Film in the Cities Gallery, St. Paul, Minnesota; *Anasazi Places*, Drake University, Des Moines, Iowa, and Blandon Art Gallery, Fort Dodge, Iowa. 1983—*Selections from High-Energy, Fusion and Space*, University of Michigan Museum of Art, Ann Arbor,

Michigan. 1984—*Selections from Most North*, Colorado College, Colorado Springs, Colorado; Fotografiska Galleriet, Oslo, Norway. 1985—Krannert Art Museum, University of Illinois, Champaign, Illinois.

Selected Group Exhibitions:

1970—Minneapolis College of Art and Design, Minneapolis, Minnesota. 1971—*Minnesota Photography*, IPOSA Exhibition, Minneapolis, Minnesota. 1973—*Images 73*, Minneapolis, Minnesota. 1974—*20th Century American Photographers*, Nelson-Atkins Museum of Art, Kansas City, Missouri. 1975—*Five Color Photographers*, Peter M. David Gallery, Minneapolis, Minnesota; *Minnesota Invitational*, Minneapolis Institute of Arts, Minneapolis, Minnesota; *Selections from the Permanent Collection*, Minneapolis Institute of Arts, Minneapolis, Minnesota. 1976—*S.P.E. Exhibit: Callahan, Morris, Torbert and Klipper*, Minneapolis Institute of Arts, Minneapolis, Minnesota; *Art of the State: State of the Art*, Minnesota Artists Exhibition Program Gallery, Minneapolis Institute of Arts, Minneapolis, Minnesota; *Photography of St. Paul*, Minnesota Museum of Art, St. Paul, Minnesota. 1978—*Selections from the Permanent Collection*, Minneapolis Institute of Arts, Minneapolis, Minnesota; Michigan Technical University, Houghton, Michigan; *Minnesota Survey: Six Photographers*, Minneapolis Institute of Arts, Minneapolis, Minnesota; *Midwestern Invitational*, John Michael Kohler Art Center, Sheboygan, Wisconsin. 1979—*8 × 10*, Susan Spiritus Gallery, Newport Beach, California. 1980—*American Photography in the 70s*, Art Institute of Chicago, Chicago, Illinois; *Working in Minnesota*, Peter M. David Gallery, Minneapolis, Minnesota. 1981—*New Landscapes*, Friends of Photography, Carmel, California. 1982—*Ranchos de Taos: An Exploration in Photographic Style, Church Photographs*, Sheldon Memorial Art Gallery, University of Nebraska, Lincoln, Nebraska; *Color as Form*, Corcoran Gallery of Art, Washington, D.C.; *Group Show*, Moderna Museet, Stockholm, Sweden; *Arteder82*, Feria Internacional de Muestras, Bilbao, Spain; *Covek i more*, International Triennial Exhibition, Zadar, Yugoslavia; *Selections from the Permanent Collection*, Museum of Modern Art, New York, New York. 1983—*An Open Land*, Art Institute of Chicago, Chicago, Illinois; *Photography and the Industrial Image*, Grey Gallery, New York University, New York, New York; *Recent Acquisitions*, Walker Art Center, Minneapolis, Minnesota. 1984—*Dolores River Project*, Colorado State Historical Society, Denver, Colorado. 1985—*Color Photography*, Williams Gallery, Denver, Colorado.

Articles and Reviews:

Gibson, Richard. "Two Photography Shows." *Minneapolis Star*, February 22, 1972, p. 8B.

Gibson, Richard. "Cameraman Limns Adult's Disneyland." *Minneapolis Star*, March 27, 1973, p. 2B.

Steele, Mike. "Minnesota Photographer." *Minneapolis Tribune*, July 17, 1975, p. 10B.

Hegeman, W. R. "6 Photographers Record Many Facets of Minnesota." *Minneapolis Tribune*, February 10, 1976, p. 7C.

Simon, Michael. *Photography*. New York: Holt, Reinhart, and Winston, 1978, p. 150.

Hegeman, W. R. "Looking at Art." *Minneapolis Tribune*, March 26, 1978, p. 10D.

Tell, Judy. "Photo Potential." *Review* (Plymouth, Wisconsin), September 19, 1978, p. 1.

Artner, Alan. "Institute Develops 3 Photography Shows." *Chicago Tribune*, February 4, 1979.

Elliot, David. "Photography." *Chicago Sun Times*, February 4, 1979, pp. 7–8.

Anderson, Phil. "Stuart Klipper—Adventurous Observer." *Minneapolis/St. Paul*, vol. 8, no. 3 (March 1980), p. 56.

Slettom, Jeanyne. "Klipper: Photographer as Philosopher." *St. Paul Dispatch*, April 17, 1980, p. 36.

Anderson, Phil. "Private Explorations." *Twin Cities Reader*, December 17, 1980, p. 23.

Houseman, William. "The Idea of North." *Architecture Minnesota*, vol. 9, no. 1 (January 1983), pp. 36–37.

Fischer, Heidi. "A Photographer's Life." *Minnesota Monthly*, vol. 17, no. 8 (August 1983), pp. 9–13.

Sneve, Arnt. "Forhekset au Polaromradene." *Arbeiderbladet* (Oslo, Norway), October 12, 1984, p. 5.

Meyer, Robert. "Kamera Studier au Naturen." *Aftenposten* (Oslo, Norway), October 26, 1984, p. 5.

Scheman, Naomi. "Photography and the Politics of Vision." *Art Paper Minneapolis*, vol. 4, no. 8 (April 1985), p. 1.

Photographs in Published Sources:

Koshalak, Richard. *Midwest Invitational*. Minneapolis, Minnesota: Walker Art Center, 1973, pp. 18, 62–63.

Maddox, Jerald. *Metamorphose Two*. St. Paul, Minnesota: Minnesota Museum of Art, 1976, pp. 3, 25.

Seitz, Peter, ed. *Minnesota Mosaic: The Bicentennial in Photographs*. Minneapolis, Minnesota: Minnesota American Revolution Bicentennial Commission, 1977, p. 55.

Hartwell, C. T. *Minnesota Survey: Six Photographers*. Minneapolis, Minnesota: Minneapolis Institute of Arts, 1978.

"Memorial Tribute to H. H. Humphrey." *Minneapolis Tribune*, January 21, 1978, p. 3A.

Hartwell, C. T. *Our Land/Our People*. St. Paul, Minnesota: First Bank and Minneapolis Institute of Arts, 1980, p. 14.

Bly, Carol. "Enemy Evenings." *Architecture Minnesota*, vol. 7, no. 3 (June 1981), pp. 55–57.

"Minnesota Worships." *Architecture Minnesota*, vol. 7, no. 6 (December 1981), pp. 38–39.

Sowder, Lynne. *Art Riches of the Upper Midwest*. Minneapolis, Minnesota: First Bank System, 1982, p. 10.

McKinney, Rhondall. *An Open Land*. Chicago, Illinois: Art Institute of Chicago, 1983, pp. 62–63.

Sowder, Lynne. *RepublicBank Houston Art Collection Catalogue*. Houston, Texas: RepublicBank, 1983, p. 28.

Hartwell, C. T. *The Making of a Collection*. Millerton, New

York: Aperture, Inc., 1984, p. 150.

Paddock, Eric. "The Dolores River Dam Project." *Colorado Heritage News*, May 1984, p. 3.

Collections:

Alexander and Alexander, Minneapolis, Minnesota; Art Institute of Chicago, Chicago, Illinois; Amon Carter Museum, Fort Worth, Texas; Chase Manhattan Art Program, New York, New York; Cray Research, Inc., Minneapolis, Minnesota; Dayton Corporation, Minneapolis, Minnesota; Delloite, Haskell, and Sells, Inc., Minneapolis, Minnesota; Dorsey Brothers Law Firm, Minneapolis, Minnesota; Exchange National Bank of Chicago, Chicago, Illinois; Faegre and Benson, Minneapolis, Minnesota; Fermi National Accelerator Laboratory, Batavia, Illinois; Film in the Cities Collection, St. Paul, Minnesota; First Bank Systems, Minneapolis, Minnesota; First National Bank, St. Paul, Minnesota; General Mills, Minneapolis, Minnesota; Jack Glenn Gallery Collection, Corona del Mar, California; Simms Grant Collection, New York, New York; Robert Israel Collection, Los Angeles, California; Kitzenberg Collection, Minneapolis, Minnesota; David and Reva Logan Foundation Collection, Chicago, Illinois; Maurer Collection, Ann Arbor, Michigan; Minneapolis Institute of Arts, Minneapolis, Minnesota; Minnesota Museum of Art, St. Paul, Minnesota; Moderna Museet, Stockholm, Sweden; Joseph Monson Collection, Seattle, Washington; Museum of Fine Arts, Houston, Texas; Museum of Fine Arts, Boston, Massachusetts; Museum of Modern Art, New York, New York; Photography Collection, Harry Ransom Humanities Research Center, University of Texas, Austin, Texas; Piper, Jaffrey, and Hopwood, Inc., Minneapolis, Minnesota; RepublicBank, Houston, Texas; Robbins, Zell, Kaplan, Inc., Minneapolis, Minnesota; St. Jude Hospital, St. Paul, Minnesota; Signode Corporation, Chicago, Illinois; Spencer Museum of Art, University of Kansas, Lawrence, Kansas; University Art Museum, University of Minnesota, Minneapolis, Minnesota; University of Michigan Museum of Art, Ann Arbor, Michigan; Walker Art Center, Minneapolis, Minnesota; Weil Collection, Washington, D.C.; Western Life Insurance Company, St. Paul, Minnesota.

Tank farm, Du Pont
Polyvinyl Alcohol
Plant, Deer Park,
1984.

All photographs are Type C color prints.

Beneath acid
vaporizer, Gulf
Coast chemical
plant, 1984.

Pipes, loading area,
Du Pont Vinyl
Acetate Plant,
Deer Park, 1984.

148

Looking out from
loading area, Du
Pont Vinyl Acetate
Plant, Deer Park,
1984.

Valves at base of
crude storage tank,
Du Pont Methanol
Complex, La Porte,
1984.

150

Hitchcock Bayou
from I-75,
Galveston County,
1984.

Box car, off Port
Industrial Boulevard,
Port of Galveston,
1984.

Tractor Trailers off
Port Industrial
Boulevard,
Port of Galveston,
1984.

Beth Jacob
Synagogue,
Galveston, 1984.

VFW Post,
24th Street,
Galveston, 1984.

[George Krause photographed urban Texas. He has chosen not to submit a statement.]

George Krause

Place of Birth: Philadelphia, Pennsylvania; January 24, 1937.

Residence: Houston, Texas.

Education: Philadelphia College of Art, Philadelphia, Pennsylvania, 1954–1957, 1959–1960.

Professional Experience:

Teaching assistant to Jerome Kaplan's lithography class, Samuel S. Fleisher Art Memorial, Philadelphia, Pennsylvania, 1958–1959; Instructor, painting and drawing, Swarthmore College, Swarthmore, Pennsylvania, 1958–1959; Instructor of photography, Samuel S. Fleisher Art Memorial, Philadelphia, Pennsylvania, 1970–1972; Instructor of photography, Brooklyn College, Brooklyn, New York, 1972–1973; Associate professor, Head of Photography Department, Bucks County Community College, Newtown, Pennsylvania, 1973–1975; Professor, Head of Photography Area, Department of Art, University of Houston, Houston, Texas, 1975–present; Associate professor, Instituto Allende, San Miguel de Allende, Mexico, Summer 1978; Director, *Venezia '79—La Fotografia* (Venice Photographic Biennale), Venice, Italy, Summer 1979.

Recognitions and Awards:

Fulbright-Hays Fellowship, 1963; Guggenheim Fellowship, 1967, 1976–1977; Philadelphia College of Art Alumni Award, 1970; National Endowment for the Arts Photography Fellowship, 1972, 1979–1980; Commission from Bicentennial Commission, Philadelphia, Pennsylvania, 1975; Prix de Rome, 1976–1977; Photographer in Residence, American Academy in Rome, Italy, 1979–1980; Unicolor Grant, 1983.

Selected Individual Exhibitions:

1970—Museo de Bellas Artes, Caracas, Venezuela. 1971-Moravian College, Bethlehem, Pennsylvania; Photographer's Place,

Berwyn, Pennsylvania. 1972—Pennsylvania State University, College Park, Pennsylvania; International Museum of Photography at the George Eastman House, Rochester, New York; Witkin Gallery, New York, New York. 1973—Pennsylvania Academy of the Fine Arts, Philadelphia, Pennsylvania; Briar Cliff College, New York, New York. 1974—Photopia Gallery, Philadelphia, Pennsylvania; Gallery of Photography, Vancouver, British Columbia, Canada; Museo de Bellas Artes, Caracas, Venezuela. 1975—Print Club, Philadelphia, Pennsylvania. 1976—Photopia Gallery, Philadelphia, Pennsylvania; Museo de Bellas Artes, Bogota, Colombia; Afterimage Gallery, Dallas, Texas; Cronin Gallery, Houston, Texas; Enjay Gallery, Boston, Massachusetts. 1977—The Photography Gallery, Vancouver, British Columbia, Canada; American Academy in Rome, Rome, Italy; *An Exhibition of Three Series*, American Academy in Rome, Rome, Italy. 1978—Witkin Gallery, New York, New York; Museum of Fine Arts, Houston, Texas. 1979—Milwaukee Center for Photography, Milwaukee, Wisconsin. 1982—Pennsylvania Academy of Fine Arts, Philadelphia, Pennsylvania. 1983—Chrysler Museum, Norfolk, Virginia.

Selected Group Exhibitions:

1963—*Five Unrelated Photographers*, Museum of Modern Art, New York, New York. 1964—*The Photographer's Eye*, Museum of Modern Art, New York, New York; *Six Photographers #1*, International Museum of Photography at George Eastman House, Rochester, New York. 1965—*Recent Acquisitions*, Museum of Modern Art, New York, New York. 1971—*Five Young Americans*, Museum of Modern Art, New York, New York. 1975—*Photography in America*, Whitney Museum of American Art, New York, New York. 1977—*Annual Exhibit*, American Academy in Rome, Italy; Galveston Art Museum, Galveston, Texas. 1978—*Mirrors and Windows: Photography since 1960*, Museum of Modern Art, New York, New York. 1979—*Self as Subject*, Scudder Gallery, Durham, New Hampshire. 1980—*Annual Exhibit*, American Academy in Rome, Rome, Italy. 1981—*New Directions: The Nude*, Massachusetts Institute of Technology, Cambridge, Massachusetts; *Salute! Five Houston Artists*, Houston Festival '81/Alley Theater, Houston, Texas; Washington Project for the Arts, Washington, D.C.

Monographs:

George Krause I. Philadelphia: Toll-Armstrong, 1972.

Portfolios:

Saints and Martyrs. Introduction by Carol Kismaric. Philadelphia: Photopia Gallery, 1976.
George Krause 1960–1970. Introduction by Mark Power. Philadelphia: Photopia Gallery, 1980.

Articles by Krause:

"Intensification." *Darkroom*. New York: Lustrum Press, 1977, pp. 105–115.
"George Krause." *Contact*. New York: Lustrum Press, 1980.
"Paper Tiger." *Camera Arts*, vol. 1, no. 2 (March/April 1981),

pp. 94–95.

Articles and Reviews:

Johnson, Patricia C. "Lively Arts: The Artist." *Houston Chronicle Zest*, August 6, 1984, p. 14.

Photographs in Published Sources:

Maloney, Tom, ed. *Photography Annual*. New York: U.S. Camera Publishing Corporation, 1962, p. 142.

Maloney, Tom, ed. *U.S. Camera International Annual*. New York: U.S. Camera Publishing Corporation, 1963, p. 174.

"George Krause, photographer." *Art in America*, vol. 51, no. 3 (June 1963), pp. 54–55.

Newhall, Beaumont. "Reality/USA." *Art in America*, vol. 52, no. 6 (December 1964), p. 91.

Szarkowski, John. *The Photographer's Eye*. New York: Museum of Modern Art, 1966, p. 68.

Durniak, John, ed. *Photography Annual*. New York: Ziff-Davis, 1966, pp. 166–171. (Portfolio)

Calendar. New York: Museum of Modern Art, 1967, photograph facing February 12.

Durniak, John, ed. *Photography Annual*. New York: Ziff-Davis, 1968, pp. 112–113. (Portfolio)

Durniak, John, ed. *Photography Annual*. New York: Ziff-Davis, 1970. (Portfolio)

The Print. New York: Time-Life Books, 1970, pp. 142–143.

The Great Themes. New York: Time-Life Books, 1970, p. 21.

Light and Film. New York: Time-Life Books, 1970, p. 38.

Stevens, Carol. "Saints, Martyrs and Everyday Mysteries." *Print*, vol. 24, no. 6 (November/December 1970), pp. 44–51. (Portfolio)

The Art of Photography. New York: Time-Life Books, 1971, pp. 100–101, 224.

Photographing Children. New York: Time-Life Books, 1971, pp. 18, 114, 210–213. (Portfolio)

"Best U.S. Posters of the Decade." *Print*, vol. 25, no. 4 (July/August 1971), pp. 36, 60.

Szarkowski, John. *Looking at Photographs: 100 Pictures from the Collection of the Museum of Modern Art*. New York: Museum of Modern Art, 1973, pp. 186–187.

Korn, Jerry, ed. "Krause's Favorites." *Photography Year 1973*. New York: Time-Life Books, 1973, pp. 160–162.

Durniak, John, ed. *Photography Annual*. New York: Ziff-Davis, 1974. (Portfolio)

Wainwright, Nicholas B., ed. *Sculpture of a City: Philadelphia's Treasures in Bronze and Stone*. New York: Walker Publishing Company, 1974.

Calendar. Philadelphia: Philadelphia Museum of Art, 1974.

Calendar. New York: Museum of Modern Art, 1975.

Mason, Jerry. *Family of Children*. New York: Grosset & Dunlap, 1977, p. 189.

Szarkowski, John. *Mirrors and Windows: American Photography since 1960*. New York: Museum of Modern Art, 1978, p. 37.

Witkin, Lee D., and Barbara London. *The Photograph Collector's Guide*. Boston: New York Graphic Society, 1979, pp. 175–176.

Venezia '79—La Fotografia. Milan, Italy: Electa, 1979. (Portfolio)

Daho, Sergio. *Il Fotografo*, anno 3, no. 33 (November 1979), pp. 40–47. (Portfolio)

Kismaric, Susan. *American Children*. New York: Museum of Modern Art, 1980, pp. 31–32.

Minkkinen, Arno. *New American Nudes*. New York: Morgan and Morgan, 1981, pp. 3–6. (Portfolio)

Houston Arts Calendar. Houston: Wordworks, Inc., 1981, page of December 7.

"Gallery: I Nudi." *American Photographer*, vol. 6, no. 4 (April 1981), p. 22.

Korn, Jerry, ed. "The Major Shows/Old Masters and New." *Photography Year 1982*. New York: Time-Life Books, 1982, pp. 80, 87.

Collections:

Addison Gallery of American Art, Andover, Massachusetts; Bibliothèque Nationale, Paris, France; Amon Carter Museum, Fort Worth, Texas; International Museum of Photography at George Eastman House, Rochester, New York; Library of Congress, Washington, D.C.; Museo de Bellas Artes, Caracas, Venezuela; Museum of Fine Arts, American Academy in Rome, Italy; Museum of Fine Arts, Boston, Massachusetts; Museum of Fine Arts, Houston, Texas; Museum of Modern Art, New York, New York; New Orleans Museum of Art, New Orleans, Louisiana; Philadelphia Museum of Art, Philadelphia, Pennsylvania; Photography Collection, Harry Ransom Humanities Research Center, University of Texas, Austin, Texas; San Antonio Museum of Art, San Antonio, Texas.

Pennzoil Building,
Houston, 1984.

All photographs are gelatin silver prints.   161

NASA, 1984.

162

kmuse

Downtown Houston,
1984.

Parking Garage,
Houston, 1984.

164

Houston, 1984.

610 Loop East,
Houston, 1984.

166

Downtown Dallas,
1984.

167

Concrete Bayous,
1984.

168

Off 610 Loop West,
Houston, 1984.

169

Galveston, 1984.

ave bonar

Can paradise be found in Texas? More particularly, can paradise be found on the largely flat and fertile terrain of the lower Rio Grande Valley? Can it be found in cities and towns with names like Hidalgo and Sullivan City, McAllen, Mercedes, Harlingen, and Brownsville?

The answer, of course, depends primarily on the people you ask, at what time of year, and where they were before coming to the Valley. The winter months in McAllen, for example, bring thousands of "snowbirds" from the upper midwest to spend their winters under the sun and the tropical palms of the lower Rio Grande. Hence a motel in downtown McAllen, owned and patronized mostly by snowbirds, is cheerfully called "The Paradise." But alas, another motel in McAllen, Windsor Court, shows the scars of the terrible freeze of December 1983, which wiped out citrus orchards and deci-

mated palm trees, casting a shadow on sunny faces.

Perhaps more profoundly, the Texas side of the lower Rio Grande has long been a magnet for impoverished Mexicanos seeking the "paradise" of life and work in the United States. It is these migrants who provide the labor for the vast agricultural enterprises that underpin the economy of the Valley. Not just the men but their wives and children work hard hours in the fields and packing sheds, cultivating, harvesting, and shipping an endless profusion of cantaloupes, onions, lettuce, and citrus fruits for American tables from coast to coast.

The lower Rio Grande Valley, then, if paradise, is a multicultural paradise, a border society in the truest sense of the term. Here you will find the Spanish language coexisting easily with English, the sounds of *conjunto* and *mariachi* with Willie Nelson, the spicy *fajita* with the chicken-fried steak. You will find bakers and *tortilla* makers in *barrio* hovels who believe they are rich. And you will find women at country clubs whose wealth is unmistakable—much of it drawn from the oil wells and cattle ranches abounding in the region.

Finally—on and under the bridges and trestles that cross the Rio Grande from Mexico—you will find each day a new generation of migrants in quest of "paradise," legally if possible, illegally if necessary. Some of them don't make it, and they are called, as Woody Guthrie sang in his famous song, "deportees."

Ave Bonar

Place of Birth: Lubbock, Texas; July 2, 1948.

Residence: Austin, Texas.

Education: B.J., University of Texas, Austin, Texas, 1976.

Professional Experience:

Chief photographer, *Daily Democrat*, Davis, California, 1973–74; Assistant editor, *1977 Book of Days by Austin Photographers*, O. Layman Graphics, Austin, Texas, 1977; Editor, *1978 Book of Days*, Laguna Gloria Art Museum in conjunction with O. Layman Graphics, Austin, Texas, 1978; Instructor, intermediate photography, and Special assistant, Judy Dater workshop, Lone Star Photographic Workshop, Austin, Texas, 1982; Chief photographer, world premier of Universal Studios' "Best Little Whorehouse in Texas," Austin, Texas, 1982; Staff photographer, Laguna Gloria Art Museum, Austin, Texas, 1983–present; Formed publishing company, Post That Card, Austin, Texas, 1984.

Selected Individual Exhibitions:

1973—Significant Directions Gallery, Davis, California. 1976—University of Texas, Austin, Texas; Austin Women's Center, Austin, Texas. 1980—The Darkroom, Austin, Texas. 1984—*Postcard Show*, Amdur Gallery, Austin, Texas.

Selected Group Exhibitions:

1976—University of Missouri, Columbia, Missouri. 1977—Bradford's Upstairs Gallery, Austin, Texas; Aperture Gallery, Austin, Texas. 1979—*Photo As Document*, California Institute of the Arts, Valencia, California. 1980—Trinity House, Austin, Texas. 1981—Galeria del Centro Cultural del Estado, Merida, Mexico. 1982—Texas Photographic Society, St. Edward's University, Austin, Texas. 1983—Gallery 104, Austin, Texas; *The Classical Photograph*, Boston Visual Artists Union, Boston, Massachusetts; *New Works by Four Austin Photographers*, Laguna Gloria Art Museum, Austin, Texas. 1984—Photowork Gallery, Austin, Texas; Amdur Gallery, Austin, Texas; *Patterns Exhibit*, Laguna Gloria Art Museum, Austin, Texas; Texas Department of Agriculture, Austin, Texas; *Austin Seen*, Austin History Center, Austin, Texas.

Photographs in Published Sources:

Bright, Susan. *Container*. Austin, Texas: Noumenon Press, 1976, cover.

Women in Texas History. Austin, Texas: People's History in Texas, 1976, n.p. (Calendar)

1977 Book of Days by Austin Photographers. Austin, Texas: O. Layman Graphics, 1977, n.p. (Calendar)

1978 Book of Days. Austin, Texas: Laguna Gloria Art Museum in conjunction with O. Layman Graphics, 1978, n.p. (Calendar)

Equitable Life Assurance Society. New York: Equitable Life Assurance Society, 1979, n.p. (Calendar)

1980 Texas Craft Exhibition. Round Top, Texas: Winedale Historical Center, 1980.

1980 Book of Days. Austin, Texas: O. Layman Graphics, 1980, n.p. (Calendar)

Pawn Review, vol. 4, no. 1 (1980–1981), pp. 30, 53.

Ulrich Ruckriem. Fort Worth, Texas: Fort Worth Art Museum, 1981, cover, p. 4.

First Federal Savings. Austin, Texas: First Federal Savings, 1981, n.p. (Calendar)

Book of Days. Austin, Texas: Light Alliance of Texas, 1981, n.p. (Calendar)

Pawn Review, vol. 5 (1981–1982), pp. 33, 125.

1981 Book of Days. Austin, Texas: Dan Schweers, 1983, n.p. (Calendar)

1984 New Works. Austin, Texas: Laguna Gloria Art Museum, 1984.

Collections:

Amon Carter Museum, Fort Worth, Texas; Museum of Fine Arts, Houston, Texas; Photography Collection, Harry Ransom Humanities Research Center, University of Texas, Austin, Texas.

bonar

Paradise Motel,
McAllen, 1984.

All photographs are gelatin silver prints.

bonar

Windsor Court,
McAllen, 1984.

175

bonar

United Farm
Workers State
Headquarters,
San Juan, 1984.

176

Adalberto y
Hermilia, Alamo,
1984.

bonar

La Estrella Bakery,
McAllen, 1984.

178

Cantaloupe Packer,
Griffin and Brand
Packing Shed,
Rio Grande City,
1984.

bonar

Cimarron Country
Club, McAllen,
1984.

180

Woman at a Tea,
McAllen, 1984.

bonar

Illegals Crossing
under Bridge,
Brownsville, 1984.

182

bonar

Deportees in
Custody of Border
Patrol, Brownsville,
1984.

183

frank gohlke

These photographs, taken together, compose a story, but only a kind of story. There is no narrative, no plot, but the order of the pictures is crucial to the meaning of the whole and its parts. The captions are essential as well, because they locate the images in a specific place and time, and ground those images in the particularities of an individual life history. What is the story about? Centers and boundaries, scale, memory, love. It is about the look of a place, about the persistence of the past in the appearance of the present. It is about me. At times it seems to me enough that the story be coherent and plausible, like any other work of fiction, since a viewer has no way of knowing whether it is true or false.

But this is too easy. Despite current theories to the contrary, it is clear that the world exists independent of our perception of it; and I believe that it is worthwhile to seek the truth of a thing, even if the enterprise is compromised by the fact that we unavoidably act upon what we observe, that perception and desire are always comingled. My affection for the north Texas landscape is neither blind nor perverse; I know that by conventional standards of scenic beauty it is an unlovely place. But there is something about its hard-bitten and scruffy vegetation that suggests survival in the face of discouraging odds. (That the foliage so often seems luxuriant up close is more an index of our low expectations of the place than anything else.) And the easy access, visual and physical, to distant horizons tantalizes us with the lure of the unbounded. Because so much of the terrain just goes on and on, the little hills, buttes, and outcrops, the gullies, washes, and rivers are correspondingly more momentous, containing hints of undisclosed possibility. It is fertile territory for tellers of tales and provides good hiding spots for the muse.

My hopes for these photographs are two: that they are accurate, in the sense that important features that characterize the landscape are represented in proper relationship to each other; and that they are persuasive, in that whatever beauty is found in the pictures does not seem to have been won at the expense of the facts.

Frank Gohlke

Place of Birth: Wichita Falls, Texas; April 3, 1942.

Residence: Minneapolis, Minnesota.

Education: B.A., University of Texas, Austin, Texas, 1964; M.A., Yale University, New Haven, Connecticut, 1967; Studied with Paul Caponigro, 1967–1968.

Recognitions and Awards:

Minnesota State Arts Council Visual Arts Fellowship, 1973; Commission from Joseph E. Seagram and Sons, Inc., Bicentennial Project, *The County Courthouse in America*, 1975–1976; Guggenheim Foundation Fellowship, 1975–1976, 1984–1985; National Endowment for the Arts Photography Survey Grant: Minnesota Survey Project, 1976–1977; National Endowment for the Arts Photographer's Fellowship, 1977–1978; Commission from AT&T Bell System American Photography Project, *American Images*, 1978; Bush Foundation Artist's Fellowship, 1979–1980; Commission from Tulsa Airport Trust to produce a series of photographic murals for the Tulsa International Airport, 1980–1981; McKnight Foundation/Film in the Cities Photography Fellowship, 1983; *Who's Who in America*, 1984.

Selected Individual Exhibitions:

1969—Johnson Gallery, Middlebury College, Middlebury, Vermont. 1971—Underground Gallery, New York, New York. 1974—International Museum of Photography at George Eastman House, Rochester, New York. 1975—Light Gallery, New York, New York; Frank Gohlke Photographs, Amon Carter Museum, Fort Worth, Texas. 1977—Viterbo College, La Crosse, Wisconsin; Boston Museum School, Boston, Massachusetts. 1978—Sheldon Memorial Art Gallery, University of Nebraska, Lincoln, Nebraska; Light Gallery, New York, New York; Museum of Modern Art, New York, New York. 1980—University Gallery, University of Massachusetts, Amherst, Massachusetts; Carleton College, Northfield, Minnesota. 1981—Light Gallery, New York, New York; Friends of Photography, Carmel, California; Memorial Art Gallery, University of Rochester, Rochester, New York; University of Tulsa, Tulsa, Oklahoma. 1982—*Aftermath: The Wichita Falls Tornado*, Light Gallery, New York, New York; Northlight Gallery, Arizona State University, Tempe, Arizona. 1983—*Mt. St. Helens: Work in Progress*, Museum of Modern Art, New York, New York; Daniel Wolf Gallery, New York, New York. 1984—*Aftermath: The*

Wichita Falls, Texas Tornado, Blue Sky Gallery, Portland, Oregon.

Selected Group Exhibitions:

1970—*Contemporary Photographers VI*, International Museum of Photography at George Eastman House, Rochester, New York. 1972—*60's Continuum*, International Museum of Photography at George Eastman House, Rochester, New York. 1973—*Photographers: Midwest Invitational*, Walker Art Center, Minneapolis, Minnesota. 1974—Two-person show with Edward Ranney, Art Institute of Chicago, Chicago, Illinois; *Light and Substance*, University of New Mexico, Albuquerque, New Mexico. 1975—*12 Photographers: Minnesota Invitational*, Minneapolis Institute of Arts, Minneapolis, Minnesota; *Young American Photographers*, Kalamazoo Institute of Arts, Kalamazoo, Michigan; *New Topographics*, International Museum of Photography at George Eastman House, Rochester, New York. 1976—*Photography for Collectors*, Museum of Modern Art, New York, New York; *Contemporary Photographic Arts*, Rio Hondo College, Whittier, California; *Recent American Still Photography*, Fruitmarket Gallery of the Scottish Arts Council, Edinburgh, Scotland; *Six American Photographers*, Thomas Gibson Fine Arts, Ltd., London, England. 1977—*Court House*, Art Institute of Chicago, Chicago, Illinois (originated by the American Federation for the Arts, New York, New York). 1978—*Minnesota Survey: Six Photographers*, Minneapolis Institute of Arts, Minneapolis, Minnesota; *Mirrors and Windows: American Photography since 1960*, Museum of Modern Art, New York, New York. 1979—*Photographers of the '70's*, Art Institute of Chicago, Chicago, Illinois; *Industrial Sites*, Whitney Museum of American Art Downtown, New York, New York; *American Images: New Work by Twenty Contemporary Photographers*, Corcoran Gallery of Art, Washington, D.C.; *Attitudes: Photography in the 1970's*, Santa Barbara Museum of Art, Santa Barbara, California. 1980—*Process and Ideology*, California Museum of Photography, Riverside, California; *New Landscapes, Part II*, Friends of Photography, Carmel, California. 1981—*American Landscapes*, Museum of Modern Art, New York, New York; *Photography: A Sense of Order*, Institute of Contemporary Art—University of Pennsylvania, Philadelphia, Pennsylvania; Two-person show with Nicholas Nixon, Kalamazoo Institute of Arts, Kalamazoo, Michigan. 1982—*New American Photography*, University of Colorado, Denver, Colorado. 1983—*Radical/Rational Space/Time*, Henry Art Gallery, University of Washington, Seattle, Washington; *An Open Land: Photographs of the Midwest 1852–1982*, Art Institute of Chicago, Chicago, Illinois; *Mt. St. Helens: The Photographer's Response*, Friends of Photography, Carmel, California; *The End of the World: Contemporary Visions of the Apocalypse*, New Museum of Contemporary Art, New York, New York.

Articles and Reviews:

Coleman, A. D. "Latent Image." *Village Voice*, October 28, 1971, pp. 35–36.

West, Stephen. "Report from the Provinces." *Village Voice*,

February 10, 1975, pp. 83–84.

Ratcliff, Carter. "Route 66 Revisited: The New Landscape Photography." *Art in America*, vol. 64, no. 1 (January–February 1976), pp. 86–91.

Lifson, Ben. "Frank Gohlke's Entrance into the Provinces." *Village Voice*, May 8, 1978, p. 80.

Hegeman, William R. "Artist with camera discovers hospitable climate in Minnesota." *Minneapolis Tribune*, October 1, 1978, pp. 1D, 8D.

Klein, Sami. "Showing an America of Wheat and Wheaties." *Minneapolis Star*, June 16, 1979, pp. 12–13.

Picard, Peter. "Midwestern Icons." *Minnesota Daily*, October 26, 1979, p. 10AE.

Pretzer, Michael. "Frank Gohlke, Chester Michalik." *Views: A New England Journal of Photography*, vol. 1, no. 4 (Summer 1980), p. 26.

Adams, Robert. *Beauty in Photography: Essays in Defense of Traditional Values.* New York: Aperture, 1981, pp. 99–102.

Grundberg, Andy. "Reflecting the Supremacy of Nature." *New York Times*, March 28, 1982, pp. 35, 38.

Karmel, Pepe. "Frank Gohlke at Light." *Art in America*, vol. 70, no. 11 (December 1982), p. 128.

"Frank Gohlke." *Aperture*, no. 93 (1983), pp. 66–67.

Thornton, Gene. "For this Subject, a Stark Documentary Style Is Right." *New York Times*, November 13, 1983, p. 31.

Edwards, Owen. "In the Valley of the Shadow." *American Photographer*, vol. 12, no. 1 (January 1984), pp. 22, 24.

French, Christopher. "Comparisons across Time." *Artweek*, vol. 15, no. 10 (March 10, 1984).

Photographs in Published Sources:

Gassan, Arnold. *A Chronology of Photography.* Athens, Ohio: Handbook Company, 1972, p. 143.

Jenkins, William. "Some Thoughts on 60's Continuum." *Image*, vol. 15, no. 1 (March 1972), p. 25.

Photographers: Midwest Invitational. Minneapolis: Walker Art Center, 1973, n.p.

Exposure, vol. 11, no. 3 (August 1973), back cover.

Light and Substance. Albuquerque: University of New Mexico, 1974, p. 14.

Camera, vol. 53, no. 10 (October 1974), p. 37.

New Topographics. Rochester, New York: International Museum of Photography at George Eastman House, 1975, pp. 24–27.

Camera, vol. 55, no. 5 (May 1976), pp. 12–17. (Portfolio)

Set of 25 slides, untitled. Rochester, New York: Light Impressions Corporation, 1977.

Lifson, Ben. *Photographs.* El Cajon, California: Grossmont College, 1977, introductory essay.

Szarkowski, John. *Mirrors and Windows: American Photography since 1960.* New York: Museum of Modern Art, 1978, p. 148.

Minnesota Survey: Six Photographers. Minneapolis: Minneapolis Institute of Arts, 1978, n.p.

Pare, Richard, ed. *Court House.* New York: Horizon Press, 1978, plates 92, 116–117, 120, 137, 152, 247, 256, 353.

Kelly, Jain, ed. *Darkroom 2*. New York: Lustrum Press, 1978, pp. 25–35.

Swanson, Mary Virginia. "Frank Gohlke: An Interview." *Northlight*, vol. 10 (1979), entire issue.

Danese, Renato, ed. *American Images: New Work by 20 Contemporary Photographers*. New York: McGraw-Hill, 1979, pp. 110–119.

"Silos of Life . . ." *New York Times*, January 18, 1979, p. 21A.

"A Photographer's View of Grain Elevators." *GTA Digest* (March–April 1979), pp. 20–23.

Adams, Robert. "Reconciliation with Geography." *Aperture*, no. 86 (1982), pp. 40–51.

An Open Land: Photographs of the Midwest, 1852–1982. Chicago: Art Institute of Chicago, 1983, pp. 46, 75.

Radical/Rational Space/Time: Idea Networks in Photography. Seattle: Henry Art Gallery, University of Washington, 1983, pp. 14–15, 30–31, 34–37.

The End of the World: Contemporary Visions of the Apocalypse. New York: New Museum of Contemporary Art, 1983, pp. 16–17.

Video:

Prairie Castles, 1/2-hour special for KTCA, Twin Cities Public Television. Produced by Mark Lowry, written and directed by Frank Gohlke and Mark Lowry, October, 1979.

Collections:

Art Institute of Chicago, Chicago, Illinois; Australian National Gallery, Canberra, Australia; California Museum of Photography, Riverside, California; Canadian Centre for Architecture, Montreal, Quebec, Canada; Amon Carter Museum, Fort Worth, Texas; Dallas Museum of Art, Dallas, Texas; Exchange National Bank of Chicago, Chicago, Illinois; Federal Reserve Bank, Minneapolis, Minnesota; General Mills, Minneapolis, Minnesota; Institute of Contemporary Art—University of Pennsylvania, Philadelphia, Pennsylvania; International Museum of Photography at George Eastman House, Rochester, New York; Kalamazoo Institute of Arts, Kalamazoo, Michigan; David and Reva Logan Foundation, Chicago, Illinois; Minneapolis Institute of Arts, Minneapolis, Minnesota; Museum of Fine Arts, Houston, Texas; Museum of Modern Art, New York, New York; National Gallery of Canada, Ottawa, Canada; Neue Sammlung, Staatliches Museum für Angewandte Kunst, Munich, Germany; Philbrook Art Center, Tulsa, Oklahoma; Polaroid Corporation, Cambridge, Massachusetts; San Antonio Museum of Art, San Antonio, Texas; Santa Barbara Museum of Art, Santa Barbara, California; Joseph E. Seagram & Sons, Inc., New York, New York; Sheldon Memorial Art Gallery, University of Nebraska, Lincoln, Nebraska; J. B. Speed Art Museum, Louisville, Kentucky; Spencer Museum of Art, University of Kansas, Lawrence, Kansas; University of Massachusetts, Amherst, Massachusetts; University of New Mexico, Albuquerque, New Mexico; University of Tulsa, Tulsa, Oklahoma; Walker Art Center, Minneapolis, Minnesota; Wichita Falls Museum and Art Center, Wichita Falls, Texas.

gohlke

The backyard of my
parents' home,
2201 Wenonah,
Wichita Falls, Texas,
1984.

190

All photographs are gelatin silver prints.

gohlke

Playground of David
Crockett Elementary
School, where I
attended grades
1–7, Wichita Falls,
Texas, 1984.

191

gohlke

Cedar trees (marking
former house site)
on Kell Blvd.
median,
Wichita Falls, Texas,
1984.

192

Wichita River,
between Petrolia and
Charlie, Texas, 1984.

Looking south
across the Red River
near Byers, Texas,
1984.

194

gohlke

Road cut, sandstone strata looking north across Red River Valley, near Petrolia, Texas, 1984. (My grandfather's early ventures in the oil business were located near here.)

195

Ross family ranch
house near Jolly,
Texas, where my
mother spent part of
her childhood
(1919–1924), 1984.

gohlke

Storm cellar behind
the (vanished)
foreman's house,
Ross family ranch,
near Jolly, Texas,
1984.

gohlke

Willow trees beside
stock tank near
Lake Arrowhead,
outside of
Wichita Falls, Texas,
1984.

gohlke

Edge of
thunderstorm
looking south near
Dean, Texas, 1982.

199

frank armstrong

My photographs represent a visual response to the visual characteristics I have found in the rural and urban social landscape. The dictionary defines "social" as "relating to or involving, the interaction of persons" and "landscape" as "a portion of land . . . which the eye can comprehend in a single view, including all the objects so seen." My photographs combine the symbols of nature and man and result in a sometimes astonishing and enigmatic picture of life. My subjects are the obscure and the transitory. They are not hidden, but they are seldom noticed by the passerby. I also photograph that portion of the landscape that has remained somewhat unaffected by man. These more classical landscapes are explorations of form as it interacts with light. To me the social landscapes are defined by the natural landscapes. One acts as a foil for the other. My photographs are dialogues between me and my subjects; they are revelations; they are exploration. They are interpretive pictures in an attempt to give form to my visual impressions, yet they are documentary photographs in that they present a highly detailed visual record of an area or scene.

Frank Armstrong

Place of Birth: Henderson, Texas; October 10, 1935.

Residence: Mt. Laurel, New Jersey.

Education: A.A., Kilgore College, Kilgore, Texas; B.J., University of Texas, Austin, Texas.

Professional Experience:

Photographic supervisor, Texas Student Publications, Inc., Austin, Texas, 1965–1969; Instructor, Photojournalism Department, University of Texas, Austin, Texas, 1969–1973;

Chief photographer, News and Information Service, University of Texas, Austin, Texas, 1969–1979; Instructor, Photography for Publication Workshop, National Association of Vocational Technical Education Communicators, San Antonio, Texas, 1976; Instructor, Photography for Publication Workshop, Women in Communication, Austin, Texas, 1978; Instructor, Fall Color Workshop, Ruidoso, New Mexico, 1979; Guest instructor, photography seminar, University of Texas, El Paso, Texas, 1980; Photography instructor, Laguna Gloria Art Museum, Austin, Texas, 1980–1983; Instructor, Oliver Gagliani Fine Print Workshops, Virginia City, Nevada, Summers 1980–1982, 1984; Instructor, Zone System and Fine Print Workshop, Scottsdale, Arizona, 1982; Instructor, Photography for Publication Workshop, *CPL News*, Center Power and Light, Corpus Christi, Texas, 1982; Instructor, Zone System Workshop, Lone Star Photographic Workshops, Austin, Texas, 1983.

Recognitions and Awards:

Dobie-Paisano Fellowship, Texas Institute of Letters and University of Texas, Austin, Texas, 1979.

Selected Individual Exhibitions:

1974—*Out of the Corner of My Eye*, Aperture Gallery, Houston, Texas. 1979—*Land and Man*, Fine Arts Studio, University of Texas, Dallas, Texas. 1980—*Social Landscapes*, Museum of the Southwest, Midland, Texas. 1981—*New Works V*, Laguna Gloria Art Museum, Austin, Texas. 1983—*Little Prints*, Precision Camera Gallery, Austin, Texas. 1984—*Social Landscapes:*

Photographs by Frank Armstrong, Wichita Falls Museum and Art Center, Wichita Falls, Texas. 1985—*The Photographs of Frank Armstrong*, Philadelphia Art Alliance, Philadelphia, Pennsylvania; *The Southwestern Landscape*, Rockwell Museum, Corning, New York.

Exhibitions Curated by Armstrong:

1972—*Jeanne Armstrong: Retrospective*, Archer M. Huntington Art Gallery, University of Texas, Austin, Texas.

Selected Group Exhibitions:

1976—*Along Texas County Roads: Photographs of Central Texas*, Michener Gallery, University of Texas, Austin, Texas; *Exhibition of Photography*, Bradford Gallery, Austin, Texas. 1981—*States of Texas*, Allen Street Gallery, Dallas, Texas. 1982—*Group Show*, Austin Photographic Cooperative, St. Edward's University, Austin, Texas; *National Invitational Show*, Galveston Arts Center, Galveston, Texas. 1983—*Group Show*, Austin Photographic Cooperative, Gallery 104, Austin, Texas; Coos Art Museum, Coos Bay, Oregon; *The Classical Photograph*, Boston Visual Artists Union, Boston, Massachusetts; *Camera Movements*, Moore College of Art, Philadelphia, Pennsylvania; Amarillo Art Center, Amarillo, Texas.

Photographs in Published Sources:

Stokesbury, Leon. *Often in Different Landscapes*. Austin, Texas: University of Texas Press, 1976, pp. ii–iii, 11, 21, 29, 37, 49, 55, 61, 67.

Carraro, Francine. "The Paisano Fellowship." *Photographic Portfolio*, vol. 2, no. 2 (June 1979).

1980 Book of Days. Austin, Texas: O. Layman Graphics, 1980, cover photograph. (Calendar)

Collections:

Amon Carter Museum, Fort Worth, Texas; Museum of Fine Arts, Houston, Texas; New Orleans Museum of Art, New Orleans, Louisiana; Photography Collection, Harry Ransom Humanities Research Center, University of Texas, Austin, Texas; United Energy Resources, Inc., Houston, Texas.

armstrong

Dennis Yadon,
Midland County,
Texas, 5-11-84.

204   *All photographs are gelatin silver prints.*

Yellow Jacket
Drive-In,
Kermit, Texas,
5-9-84.

205

armstrong

AF & AM Lodge,
Grandfalls, Texas,
5-12-84.

Stanton, Texas,
5-8-84.

Smelter Cemetery,
El Paso, Texas,
5-17-84.

Elmer Hunt, Larry
Hunt, Todd Hunt,
Ward County, Texas,
5-12-84.

San Francisco de
Assis, El Paso
County, Texas,
5-16-84.

Texas Highway 20,
El Paso County,
Texas, 5-16-84.

211

armstrong

Andrews, Texas,
5-8-84.

212

armstrong

Texas Highway 158,
Midland County,
Texas, 5-8-84.

213

gay block

The energy of my life seems to depend on my relationship with people, so that must be the reason I do portraits. Photography's worst aspect is the fact of having to work alone; at least I don't have to be alone while I photograph.

These portraits of artists represent a departure from my earlier work. I have never before impressed so much of myself on my photographs, but I got very involved in these people as artists and couldn't resist making some portraits echo their work.

Gay Block

Place of Birth: Houston, Texas; March 5, 1942.

Residence: Houston, Texas.

Education: Sophie Newcomb College, New Orleans, Louisiana, 1959–1961; School of Architecture, University of Houston, Houston, Texas, 1971–1972; Studied with Geoff Winningham, Garry Winogrand, and Anne Tucker, 1973–1976.

Professional Experience:

Instructor, University of Houston, Houston, Texas, 1979–1980, 1982–1983.

Recognitions and Awards

National Endowment for the Arts Photographers Fellowship, 1978; National Endowment for the Arts Photography Survey Grant, *The Ties That Bind: Photographers Portray the Family*, under the auspices of "Women and Their Work," Austin, Texas, 1981.

Selected Individual Exhibitions:

1977—Portland School of Art, Portland, Maine. 1979—Cronin Gallery, Houston, Texas. 1981—University of Houston, Clear Lake, Texas. 1982—Contemporary Arts Museum, Houston, Texas. 1984—Twin City Art Foundation, Monroe, Louisiana. 1985—Graham Gallery, Houston, Texas; Dillingham Center, Ithaca College, Ithaca, New York.

Selected Group Exhibitions:

1975—*Breadth of Vision: Portfolios of Women Photographers*, Fashion Institute of Technology, New York, New York. 1977—*Images of Women*, Portland Museum of Art, Portland, Maine; *Four Texas Photographers*, Fort Worth Art Museum, Fort Worth, Texas. 1979—*Anthony G. Cronin Memorial Exhibition*, Museum of Fine Arts, Houston, Texas. 1980—*U.S. Eye*, Winter Olympics, Lake Placid, New York; *Response*, Tyler Museum of Art, Tyler, Texas; *SECA Invitational*, San Francisco Museum of Modern Art, San Francisco, California; *Triennial*, New Orleans Museum of Art, New Orleans, Louisiana. 1981—*Texas Photographers*, Washington Project for the Arts, Washington, D.C.; *Inside/Out: The Self Beyond Likeness*, Newport Harbor Art Museum, Newport Beach, California; *The Ties That Bind: Photographers Portray the Family*, Dougherty Cultural Arts Center, Austin, Texas. 1982—*Houston in Stavanger*, Stavanger, Norway/Houston, Texas; *Women's Caucus for Art Exchange Exhibition*, Philadelphia, Pennsylvania. 1983—*Film and Photo Exhibition*, Santa Fe Center for Photography, Santa Fe, New Mexico; Houston Center for Photography, Houston, Texas. 1984—Boston University Art Gallery, Boston, Massachusetts. 1985—*The Family*, Katherine E. Nash Gallery, University of Minnesota, Minneapolis, Minnesota.

Articles and Reviews:

Kalil, Susie. "Portrait of a Community." *Artweek*, vol. 10, no. 22 (June 16, 1979), p. 12.

Johnson, Patricia C. "Ordinary People, Compelling Photos." *Houston Chronicle*, May 23, 1982, p. 17.

Lippman, Marcia. "The Question of Beauty." *Ms.*, vol. 11, no. 11 (May 1983), p. 78.

Barry, Margaret. "American Assignments." *Views: A New England Journal of Photography*, vol. 6, no. 1 (Winter 1985), p. 14.

Photographs in Published Sources:

Camera, vol. 56, no. 8 (August 1977), p. 10.

Alinder, James, ed. *Self-Portrayal*. Carmel, California: Friends of Photography, 1979, n.p.

Video/Film:

A Tribute to Spirit: The Beth Israel Experience, 16-mm film, Houston Public Television, KUHT, April 17, 1976.

A bie gesunt. 30-minute video about the Jews of South Beach, Miami, Florida, produced by Gay Block, 1984.

Collections:

Amon Carter Museum, Fort Worth, Texas; Center for Creative Photography, Tucson, Arizona; Anthony G. Cronin Memorial Collection, Museum of Fine Arts, Houston, Texas; Fort Worth Art Museum, Fort Worth, Texas; Museum of Fine Arts, Houston, Texas; Photography Collection, Harry Ransom Humanities Research Center, University of Texas, Austin, Texas; Portland Museum of Art, Portland, Maine.

They had had a nice time together, but she knew that their goodbye would be a handshake and not a kiss.

Vernon Fisher.
Fort Worth, 1984.

block

All photographs are gelatin silver prints.

Nic Nicosia. Dallas,
1984. [Triptych]

block

Lee Smith. Dallas,
1984.

219

Luis Jiménez.
El Paso, 1984.

220

block

Ed and Linda
Blackburn.
Fort Worth, 1984.

221

block

Jim Love. Houston, 1984.

222

block

Melissa Miller.
Austin, 1984.

223

block

James Surls with
Lillie. Splendora,
1984.

224

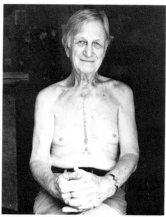

RUSSELL LEE, FISHERMAN, POLITICAL ACTIVIST, PHOTOGRAPHER

RUSSELL'S 1982 OPEN HEART SURGERY SCAR

RUSSELL LEE IN HIS BACK YARD AUSTIN, TX 1984

Russell Lee. Austin, 1984.

Gael Stack.
Houston, 1984.

skeet mcauley

Since 1978 my work has been a color investigation of the contemporary landscape. This work with the 4″ × 5″ view camera began with the "Barriers Series," which was the impetus for several ongoing series that are both complementary and overlapping. These include the "Wildlife Series," the "Tree Series," and the "Manscape Series." All of these give analogous attention to our relationship with the natural environment.

My most recent work, the "Native American Series," is a contemporary view of the cultures that have traditionally considered the land sacred. These pictures consider the figure as an element of the landscape. It is this addition of the figure that inspired the "Workperson Series" for my part of *Contemporary Texas: A Photographic Portrait*. Looking at the relatively new cities of Dallas and Fort Worth it is easy to forget the human element involved in their construction and maintenance.

The workpersons were photographed with peripheral concern for their working environment. It is this juxtaposition of the human element with the environment that continues to interest me.

Skeet McAuley

Place of Birth: Monahans, Texas; March 7, 1951.

Residence: Dallas, Texas.

Education: B.A., Sam Houston State University, Huntsville, Texas, 1976; M.F.A., Ohio University, Athens, Ohio, 1978.

Professional Experience:

Teaching assistant, Ohio University, Athens, Ohio, 1976–1978; Initiated *Project Discovery*, a program using the camera as a communication tool for mentally retarded adults, Athens Mental Health Center, Athens, Ohio, 1977–1978; Instructor of photography, Spring Hill College, Mobile, Alabama, 1978–1979; Instructor of photography, Tyler Junior College, Tyler, Texas, 1979–1981; Assistant professor of photography, North Texas State University, Denton, Texas, 1981–present.

Recognitions and Awards:

Faculty Research Grant, North Texas State University, Denton, Texas, 1981, 1982; National Endowment for the Arts Photographers Fellowship, 1984; Commission from Dallas Public Library, Dallas, Texas, *Focus Dallas Project: Downtown Dallas and the Work Person*, 1984.

Selected Individual Exhibitions:

1980—Southern Light Gallery, Amarillo, Texas; Tyler Museum of Art, Tyler, Texas; Cronin Gallery, Houston, Texas. 1981—Prairie State College Art Gallery, Chicago Heights, Illinois. 1982—University of Ottawa Art Gallery, Ottawa, Canada; Mattingly Baker Gallery, Dallas, Texas. 1983—ASA Gallery, University of New Mexico, Albuquerque, New Mexico; Light Fantastic Gallery, Michigan State University, East Lansing, Michigan. 1984—University of California Extension Center, San Francisco, California.

Selected Group Exhibitions:

1979—Two-person exhibition, Fine Arts Museum of the South, Mobile, Alabama. 1980—Carpenter Center for Visual Arts, Harvard University, Cambridge, Massachusetts; *Fifth Anniversary Exhibition*, Cronin Gallery, Houston, Texas.

1981—Two-person exhibition, Hill's Gallery, Denver, Colorado; *Imagism*, Light Factory, Charlotte, North Carolina; *The Road Show Collection '81: 14 Texas Artists*, Two Houston Place, Houston, Texas; *Tenth Anniversary Exhibition*, Tyler Museum of Art, Tyler, Texas. 1982—ASA Gallery, University of New Mexico, Albuquerque, New Mexico; Foothills Art Center, Golden, Colorado; Texas Woman's University Art Gallery, Denton, Texas; Colorado Photographic Arts Center, Denver, Colorado; Galveston Art Center, Galveston, Texas; David Mancini Gallery, Houston, Texas; Museum of Art, University of Oklahoma, Norman, Oklahoma; *Southwest Exhibition*, Northlight Gallery, Arizona State University, Tempe, Arizona; California Institute for the Arts, Valencia, California; Camerawork Gallery, San Francisco, California. 1983—E. J. Bellocq Gallery, Louisiana Tech University, Ruston, Louisiana; Center for Arts and Performance, Houston, Texas; *Arboretum*, University of Denver, Denver, Colorado; Chautauqua Art Association Gallery, Chautauqua, New York; Moore College of Art, Philadelphia, Pennsylvania; *The Land Redefined*, Sioux City Art Center, Sioux City, Iowa; Art Museum of South Texas, Corpus Christi, Texas; Burlington Cultural Center, Ontario, Canada; Boston Art Institute, Boston, Massachusetts. 1984—*A Place of Order: Five Emerging Artists*, Galveston Art Center, Galveston, Texas; *The Urban Landscape*, Pacific Grove Art Center, Pacific Grove, California; *Contemporary Color*, Sioux City Art Center, Sioux City, Iowa; *The Art Elements*, Dallas Museum of Art, Dallas, Texas; *Olivia Parker, Skeet McAuley, Scogin Mayo*, Allen Street Gallery, Dallas, Texas; *Northlight/*

Southwest, Northlight Gallery, Arizona State University, Tempe, Arizona; *Jergen Strunk and Skeet McAuley*, Waco Art Center, Waco, Texas.

Collections:

Atlantic Richfield Oil Company, Dallas, Texas; Amon Carter Museum, Fort Worth, Texas; Museum of Art, University of Oklahoma, Norman, Oklahoma; North Texas State University, Denton, Texas; Permian Basin Petroleum Museum, Midland, Texas; Photography Collection, Harry Ransom Humanities Research Center, University of Texas, Austin, Texas; Republic-Bank, Dallas, Texas; R. J. Reynolds Corporation, Charlotte, North Carolina; Tyler Museum of Art, Tyler, Texas.

Workperson Series,
Perfumer or "Nose"
for Mary Kay
Cosmetics, Dallas,
1984.

All photographs are Type C color prints.

mc'nuley

Workperson Series,
Set for "Guilty or
Innocent," Dallas
Communications
Complex, Irving,
1984.

Workperson Series,
Loading Newsprint
on Press at *Dallas
Morning News,*
Dallas, 1984.

m^cauley

Workperson Series,
Concrete Workers,
Downtown Dallas,
1984.

233

mcauley

Workperson Series,
Ceiling Tile Worker
Using Laser Device
for Leveling, Dallas,
1984.

234

Workperson Series,
Southwest Airlines
Flight Trainer
Demonstrating Use
of Fire Extinguisher,
Irving, 1984.

235

mcauley

Workperson Series,
Museum Worker
with Top Portion of
Oldenburg's "Stake
Hitch," Dallas, 1984.

236

Workperson Series,
Museum Worker
with Bottom Portion
of Oldenburg's
"Stake Hitch,"
Dallas, 1984.

237

mcnuley

Workperson Series,
Crane Operator and
Steel Worker,
Downtown, Dallas,
1984.

238

mcauley

Workperson Series,
Groundskeeper,
Stockyards Arena,
Fort Worth, 1984.